PRAISE FOR *CHARISMA*

"An excellent step-by-step guide."
  **—John Gray, author of *Men Are from
  Mars, Women Are from Venus***

"A boon to anyone who needs guidance on how to make a personal connection with people. . . . There's nothing like charisma to achieve spectacular results."
  **—Daniel Burrus, author of
  *Technotrends***

"Another myth bites the dust! You don't have to be born with charisma. You can learn how to get it. . . . Tony can teach you how to do it. Great book, I loved it."
  **—Robert Kriegel, coauthor of
  *Sacred Cows Make the Best Burgers***

"All of us can become more effective at influencing others, and Tony Alessandra shows us how in this wonderful book."
  **—Michael LeBoeuf, author of *Working
  Smart* and *The Perfect Business***

"Charisma is the only item I haven't sold yet. But Tony has it and we can all gain from it. BUY THIS."
  —Kathy Levine, host, QVC, Inc.

more . . .

"Shows how all of us can ethically and effectively marshal this source of social influence for the betterment of our careers, our teams, and our organizations."
> **—Charles Garfield, Ph.D., author of**
> ***Second to None* and**
> ***Peak Performers***

"Dr. Tony Alessandra is unstoppable, and where charisma is concerned, he wrote the book! Read CHARISMA and unleash your untapped magnetism. . . . It's that good."
> **—Tod Barnhart, author of**
> ***The Five Rituals of Wealth***

"A makes-sense approach to improving one's ability to positively influence others."
> **—*Detroit Free Press***

"Well organized and clearly written . . . Alessandra's recommendations for improving public speaking and listening . . . are useful."
> **—*Publishers Weekly***

"Learn how people with charisma function and how to develop this valuable skill."
> **—*Fort Wayne Journal Gazette***

"A step-by-step program to strengthen your own abilities . . . in a way that boosts your own magnetism."
> **—*Hartford Business Journal***

"Identifies the key ingredients and offers a program of step-by-step 'charisma basics.'"
    —*Pittsburgh Business Times*

"Shares how this all-important combination of positive energy, confidence, and vision can create the kind of career and accomplishments that most people only dream about."
    —*Midwest Book Review*

"[An] essential tool for persuasive communication . . . offers a disciplined, practical approach to maximizing personal effectiveness."
    —**Dick Capen, former U.S. ambassador to Spain and publisher of the** *Miami Herald*

"Charisma! If you want more than you already have, read this fascinating and powerful book."
    —**Tom Connellan, author of** *Inside the Magic Kingdom*

CHARISMA

Seven Keys to Developing the Magnetism that Leads to Success

TONY ALESSANDRA, Ph.D.

WARNER BOOKS

A Time Warner Company

Copyright © 1998 by Tony Alessandra
All rights reserved.

Warner Books, Inc., 1271 Avenue of the Americas, New York, N.Y. 10020
Visit our Web site at www.twbookmark.com

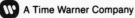 A Time Warner Company

Printed in the United States of America
First Trade printing: February 2000
10 9 8 7 6 5 4 3

The Library of Congress has cataloged the hardcover edition as follows:

Alessandra, Anthony J.
    Charisma : seven keys to developing the magnetism that leads to
    success / Tony Alessandra.
        p. cm.
    ISBN 0-446-52049-7
    1. Charisma (Personality trait) I. Title.
BF698.35.C45A44   1998
155.2'32—DC21   97-1145
                                                    CIP
    ISBN 0-446-67598-9 (pbk.)

Book design and composition by L&G McRee

For Sue, whose unconditional love and unquenchable desire to help me become the very best "me" I can be have reignited my charisma. When one is this happy and fulfilled, it's so much easier for the good traits to surface. Thank you for being such a wonderful wife, partner, friend, confidante, soul mate, and fellow adventurer. I love you passionately.

CONTENTS

———————◆———————

ACKNOWLEDGMENTS

◆

I'm indebted to many for help in bringing this book into being. First, special thanks goes to Cindy Spring, who took my material and successfully wrote the original audio script for me for the *How to Achieve Power & Influence with People* audio album produced by Nightingale-Conant. Also, I wish to thank Dale Fetherling, who played a major role in organizing and editing my material, always patiently and efficiently. Dale's writing skills and creativity shaped this book into a powerful success tool.

A number of my associates with whom I wrote earlier books again were generous with their time and ideas. Prominent among them are Rick Barrera, Phil Hunsaker, Michael O'Connor, Phil Wexler, and, especially, Jim Cathcart, who contributed content and feedback for many of these chapters.

I quote with gratitude many authors and experts,

Acknowledgments

but I particularly want to acknowledge the works of Anthony Athos, Warren Bennis, Sheila Murray Bethel, Connie Bruck, Robert Cialdini, Jay Conger, Dave Jensen, Daniel Goleman, Marcia Grad, Paul Hersey, Alec Mackenzie, Mark McCormack, George Walther, Garry Wills, Gary Yukl, and Elaina Zuker. I also wish to thank my agent, Margret McBride, and Susan Suffes, my editor at Warner Books.

During the final phases of writing, I asked many friends and colleagues, each of whom demonstrates some expertise in various aspects of charisma, for input. Their contributions are very much appreciated: Sharon Adcock, Sue Alessandra, Ron Arden, Arden Bercovitz, Jeff Blackman, Joe Calloway, Bill Cates, Roger Dawson, David Garfinkel, John Garrett, Bobby Gee, Lou Hampton, Jim Hennig, Sue Hershkowitz, Al Hops, Allan Hurst, Marita Littauer, James Melton, Bill Metcalf, George Morrisey, Sue Pistone, Ed Rigsbee, Susan RoAne, Anthony Rubbo, Mark Sanborn, Nikki Sweet, Jim Tunney, Al Walker, and Bill Weiss.

Finally, I'm grateful to all the individuals who read the manuscript and provided the powerful endorsements that appear on the covers and front pages of this book.

CHARISMA

◆

EVERYONE CAN HAVE CHARISMA IF ONLY . . .

- You walk into a room and soon notice an animated conversation among a knot of several people. You're attracted to their energy and start to join them. Then you see that one fellow has already turned and is now talking to someone else. The original group drifts apart, and that one man again quickly becomes the center of yet another high-energy group. On and on, throughout the evening, you watch him effortlessly pull others to him like moths to a flame.

  What is it about this man that attracts others so readily? How, without seeming to try, does he always end up as the center of attention?

- Or, at work, two managers with equal training and experience are put in charge of similar group tasks. But the results differ drastically. One task force flounders and misses a critical deadline. The other quickly meshes as a team and produces a report so stunning that the breadth, depth, and clarity of its ideas has everyone talking.

1

Why does one manager succeed, while her colleague fails to connect with his people? Why does one need to check and recheck his subordinates' work constantly, while the other manager just points her people in the right direction and they take off?

Those successful people aren't just lucky. What the engaging conversationalist and the superbly effective manager have in common is enormous *charisma*. But this is not an effortless gift from the gods, not necessarily something they were born with.

Instead, it's a constellation of social skills, or tools. Collectively, these qualities are sometimes also referred to as personal magnetism. You may not know it, but those qualities, those tools, are within you, too, just waiting to be developed, to be honed.

And the wonderful thing about using these skills is that they make you powerful without making others less so. That's because the kind of power I'm talking about is interpersonal influence—not the power of potentates, or generals, or other autocrats to *order* things to happen. Instead, I'm talking about the power to be effective with people. I'm talking about acquisition of power through interpersonal means, appropriate means, means that don't take power away from others but give *you and them* the power to achieve favorable outcomes.

DEVELOPING YOUR CHARISMA

But, on the other hand, nothing good comes easily. And while you have latent charisma, developing it isn't automatic. You must be motivated and prepared to spend the time and make the effort to sharpen your skills.

I've spent years studying why and how some people are viewed as more charismatic than others. This book, using examples both famous and obscure, will explain and illustrate what I believe are the most common skills of charismatic people. More important, I'm going to give you many, many suggestions on ways to develop your charisma.

First, we'll explore charisma as a whole. What are its basic ingredients? Where does the concept come from? Why is there so much confusion about it?

Then, before getting into the skills themselves, we'll speculate on why charisma is more important now than ever before. You'll see how true personal magnetism emanates from *within* you, not from your title or whether you have a corner office, not from the size of your desk or the size of your salary.

Then, starting with Chapter 3, we'll get into the seven keys to charisma. Each of those seven chapters will include a Quick Quiz, or self-assessment, for determining how you measure up now.

Of course, to have great personal magnetism, you must be an able communicator. Thus, you'll see chapters on how to improve your skills in:

- Speaking
- Listening
- Persuading
- Adapting to others

But communication is more than just what you say or how you say it. We communicate in many less obvious ways, too. You'll also learn how to:

- Send out the best "silent message," or image
- Use space and time to your advantage
- Expand your vision and ideas

In addition to the many suggestions and examples in the text, you'll find at the end of each chapter another ten ideas for "jump-starting" that particular skill. And, finally, Chapter 10, "A Last Nudge toward Being the Best You Can Be," will offer yet another ten specific ways you can maximize your charisma.

Throughout the book, you'll also be urged to get other people to tell you what they think about you. That's because there's often a gap between how we see ourselves and how others see us. You might, for example, give yourself a fairly low mark as a speaker because you know you're nervous when you give a talk. On the other hand, your audience might think you're a fine presenter. (Of course, there's always the possibility of the opposite, too: You might think you're terrific, while most everyone thinks you're a bore!)

It will be important that you ask others for feedback. And those need to be the right people, people who'll tell you the truth. You'll be looking for feedback that will add to, you might say, a 360-degree picture of yourself. So you'll need to ask for feedback from those who know you at work, at home, on the tennis court, or wherever you're mingling with others. Make sure each individual is not only candid, but also familiar with your behavior in that situation. For instance, you wouldn't ask your mother about your speaking ability in a business meeting, unless she were on the board of directors—and maybe not even then!

In short, this is a book designed to maximize your effectiveness, whether you're a CEO or a clerk, an engineer or an apprentice. We all need these skills because they help build trust and commitment. And trust and commitment are the bedrock of every successful endeavor. Without them, organizations don't function well, coalitions don't get built, collaborations don't occur, opinions and attitudes don't get changed, and careers rarely take off.

In any case, welcome aboard! Whatever your current level of charisma, if you'd really like to improve it, you've come to the right place.

PART I

---◆---

THE FOUNDATIONS
OF CHARISMA

CHAPTER 1

◆

CHARISMA: WHAT IS IT?
WHAT WILL IT DO FOR YOU?

You're sweating it out in a corporate conference room, awaiting your turn to speak. And, of course, you're trying to subtly size up your competition for this big consulting job. Then this one guy gets up to make his presentation—and, *arrghhh!* It's a Maalox moment.

He moves with such grace and confidence that the room falls silent and all heads swivel as he approaches the microphone. Looking poised and confident, he smiles, then begins. Instantly, it's clear that he's *good*—and he and everyone else in the room knows it. His strong, measured voice, his relaxed tone, his precisely articulated and well-chosen words, even his classy but understated appearance, seem to fixate the crowd.

You think, Wow! Who *is* this guy? And then you realize it's just not what he is saying, or how he looks. It's his whole being. He couldn't be more stunning if he wore a neon suit.

But you feel your envy dissolve into admiration as his words sink in. That's because he affects you and the others not just rationally but in an emotional, visceral way, too. As his cadence quickens and his voice and gestures signal that he's nearing the high point of his remarks, you feel yourself soaring along with the ideas he presents so passionately—so much so that you decide, competitor or no competitor, you'd probably follow him to a convention of cannibals if that's where he wanted to lead you. This guy *has* it!

APPEAL TO MIND AND EMOTIONS

You've probably met such people who've inspired you with their vigor and motivated you by their energy, who've appealed to your emotions as well as your mind. And you may have found yourself, quite willingly, drawn to them and perhaps performing beyond expectations to accomplish *their* goals.

But have you asked yourself: What's the source of such authority? What are its ingredients? What has so endowed these men and women with personal magnetism?

Does it come merely from speaking well? Or is it that they're socially adroit, able to adjust smoothly to any personality or situation? Or is their secret how they manage to project an attractive, exciting image that makes us feel good just being around them?

Actually, it's all of that—and much more. And for lack of a better term, we often group such qualities under the word *charisma*.

Charisma is easy to spot but hard to describe. Nailing down a definition is like trying to define America, or happiness, or what constitutes a terrific meal or a great vacation. Everybody you ask has a different idea, all of them valid, at least to themselves. And the effort is made more frustrating by the fact that we all tend to overuse the term, lavishing it indiscriminately on insolent athletes, glamorous film stars, and fanatic cultists, as well as on genuinely enchanting and inspirational personalities like, say, John F. Kennedy, Mahatma Gandhi, and Dr. Martin Luther King, Jr.

Here's my definition: *Charisma is the ability to influence others positively by connecting with them physically, emotionally, and intellectually.*

In brief, it's what makes people like you—even when they don't know much about you. This personal magnetism (a term I use interchangeably with *charisma*) can exist at the level of mass movements—such as those led by politicians and evangelists—or in the small-scale encounters of everyday life, such as the shop owner who makes you feel so comfortable and valuable that you cheerfully drive a few extra miles to her store.

Charisma at either level, writes Harvard anthropologist Charles Lindholm, involves "a compulsive, inexplicable emotional tie." While charisma, he notes, is thought of as something intrinsic to the individual, it can be revealed only in interaction with others. "Charisma is," Lindholm says, "above all, a *relationship*, a mutual mingling of the inner selves of leader and follower."

Making those connections is what makes a leader. I liken this process between the leader and the led to an energy-feedback loop. When you connect with people, energy passes both ways. If it's a powerful connection, the energy builds and builds. And when that happens, both leader and followers feel exhilarated and truly alive.

WELL WITHIN YOUR GRASP

I'm also convinced that, popular wisdom to the contrary, charisma is not something you're born with, like having blue or brown eyes. It's not in your genes—and it's not beyond your grasp. In other words, you already have charisma. But it's not configured the same way in you as it is in the person next to you.

Think of it this way: Each of our personalities consists, let's say, of a series of containers, like cups or glasses. Some are nearly empty, some brimming, yet others are partially filled to varying degrees. Together they constitute our charisma, or at least our potential charisma.

If all the glasses were filled to the top, you'd be so charismatic people would think you were a god—and you'd probably think so, too. But nobody has a complete set of totally full glasses, although some really, really gifted people may come close to this ideal.

But, for most of us, the glasses are filled a bit erratically. Maybe your glass marked *Persuasiveness* is very full, but your glass labeled *Adaptability* is bordering on empty. Or you're a good listener, but your skill at projecting a strong, exciting image is so-so.

So, everybody has glasses, but everybody's glasses are filled to differing depths. This book can help you raise some of those levels. Together, we'll work on those areas where your glass isn't very full.

Like enhancing any other set of skills, developing your charisma takes practice and hard work, which is to say that you must be motivated. "Nobody will follow a turnip," Robert B. Horton, former chairman of Standard Oil, once wrote. "To lead you need passion . . . ardor, zeal, enthusiasm—this personal involvement is absolutely necessary in a good leader."

HOPE FOR GEEKS?

Can a geek become charismatic? Can a dweeb become dashing? Yes, if he or she works on filling the right glasses.

Bill Gates, the founder of Microsoft, is not an imposing physical presence or a marvelous speaker. Yet he's clearly a leader and, some would say, charismatic. Why? Because he's extremely wealthy?

No, he's probably extremely wealthy because he is charismatic. In his case, his glass marked *Vision* or *Ideas* is filled beyond overflowing, making him an intoxicating leader. Some of his other glasses probably could use an extra dollop.

I've been studying, teaching, and writing about human behavior, especially in business, for more than twenty years now. As a professional speaker, I've observed and talked to many powerful communicators. And as a consultant to some of America's biggest firms, I've been lucky enough to watch many of the nation's top business leaders in action. As a result, probably like you, I know charisma when I see it—even if it's sometimes hard to pinpoint.

REDUCING CHARISMA TO ITS BEDROCK

Still, I've wanted to be able to describe charisma more concretely. So I've thought a lot about it, formed some opinions, and done applied research. I've also studied the literature, going back decades, and compared the conclusions of scholars with my own observations.

Though the results may not be strictly scientific, I've

13

sought to reduce charisma to its bedrock. What I've come up with are seven qualities that I'm convinced are at its core. This book looks in detail at each of them.

Here's how I see those seven main components of charisma—or, the "glasses," if you will:

- *Your silent message.* These are the signals you send out unconsciously to others. Maybe you look people right in the eye, or maybe you stare at your shoes when you talk to them. Maybe you slump your shoulders or square them confidently. Maybe you don't smile naturally or shake hands firmly, or you dress in a way that's not *you.* These can all shape your silent message, your "image."
- *Your ability to speak well.* You may have a terrific idea, but who will know if you can't articulate it?
- *Your listening skills.* Rarely taught and infrequently practiced, listening is nonetheless a key to communicating and making others feel special in your presence.
- *Your persuasive talent.* This is your skill at motivating others to follow your lead or adopt your idea. No idea, however great, ever gets anywhere until it's adopted.
- *Your use of space and time.* Again, though it's often overlooked, your use of spatial and temporal territories can make or break relationships.
- *Your ability to adapt to others.* Building bridges to others is impossible without understanding other people's personalities, then adapting your own behavior to increase rapport.
- *Your vision, your ideas.* In the final analysis, no matter how strong and persuasive a speaker you are, how adept you are at building rapport, how well you listen, use your space or time, or send out silent signals, you've *got* to have something to say—or you'll just be an empty suit.

So, to repeat, it's not a single ingredient that makes a person charismatic. The real charismatic leader has multiple skills and behaviors that are, to some extent, dependent on one another.

But the best news is that charisma isn't based on IQ, genetics, social position, wealth, or luck. Instead, it can be learned. In the core of this book, you'll learn to maximize each element of your charisma, how you can raise the levels in all your "glasses."

WHY CHARISMA MATTERS

You don't hear much about charisma in business school. But think about the really powerful leaders you've known. When people have charisma, excitement follows them, spreading out to those around them. This kind of leader galvanizes others into action.

Maybe that's why some of our fabled chieftains— Lincoln, Churchill, and Roosevelt, for instance— presided during national emergencies. Or why charismatic corporate bosses often are at their peak when the firm is searching for its identity, trying to claim or reclaim its niche.

Thus, when an outcome is in doubt, when some big decision hangs in the balance, when conditions are uncertain, that's when we look to the strong, mesmerizing leader. Since, in our Information Age, almost everything is in flux, charisma is now all the more in demand.

Add to that the fact that television and our general emphasis on the visual make charismatic people more effective. (The physical is a big component of the *Silent*

Message glass, you'll recall.) And, last, the old-fashioned kind of hierarchy, the command-and-control environment, is passé. People just don't rotely do what they're told as they might have done thirty or forty years ago. Even the highest-ranking officials need more than their title to get people to accept their ideas.

Instead, this is the era of "empowerment," when empathy and support are revered. Those are characteristics many charismatic people have in spades. They're able to see things from another's perspective and, thus, are continually trying to find the common ground.

All of these factors add up to increased importance for charisma, for cultivating within yourself the qualities that will make you stand out and make others take notice. To illustrate the point, consider a group of individuals we all know: the candidates for U.S. President over the last few decades. Admittedly, presidential politics is a complicated mix: the nation's economic health, the public's mood, the web of ideas and issues, foreign threats, the efforts of the "spin doctors"—all these play a role.

But try to isolate for a moment the role of charisma. In just about every case since 1960, the more charismatically challenged candidate has lost. John F. Kennedy defeated Richard Nixon. (Interestingly, radio listeners were convinced Nixon had won the debates with Kennedy. But those who saw the pair on TV had a decidedly different view, thus underscoring the importance of the visual element in charisma.)

Subsequently, a reinvigorated Nixon defeated bland George McGovern. Jimmy Carter, being perceived as a "human" candidate after the harsh Nixon years, beat less-than-exciting Gerald Ford. Ronald Reagan, perhaps the most charismatic of them all, coasted to two successive wins. George Bush, not a supremely charismatic man, defeated Michael Dukakis, who was even less so. Then Bill Clinton defeated Bush and easily shoved aside a challenge by the decidedly noncharismatic Bob Dole.

And those were the nominees! Think of the also-rans—some of them endowed with the charisma of an anchovy (remember Paul Tsongas or Steve Forbes?)—who didn't survive the primaries.

The only possible exceptions in almost four decades of presidential battles were Lyndon Johnson's defeat of Barry Goldwater in 1964 and Nixon's win over Hubert Humphrey four years later. Arguably, Goldwater was more charismatic. But in the wake of the Kennedy assassination, Johnson still carried some of the Kennedy mystique and, further, Goldwater was perceived, rightly or wrongly, as an extremist. In Humphrey's case, the legacy of the Vietnam War hung like a millstone around his neck.

THE MANY SHADES OF CHARISMA

I've spent much of my career selling, teaching individuals how to sell, and, in recent decades, consulting with firms about improving sales. As a result, I know for a fact there's no such thing as a "born salesperson." It's bunk to say that a certain type of person—outgoing, expressive, maybe backslapping or even domineering—can, through force of personality, sell anything to anybody.

I've seen many a top account executive who isn't particularly glib, is a bit of an introvert, never tries high-pressure tactics, and wouldn't know a fancy closing technique if you diagrammed one on a chalkboard. Yet he or she consistently sets sales records and makes the customers rave. Why?

Because the salesperson knows what he or she has got and makes the most of it. Being outgoing and expressive can be valuable attributes in a salesperson. But a lot of selling, for example, centers around what you're selling and to whom. The more reserved salesperson often does quite well selling complicated products requiring a long-term commitment like, say, communication networks or computer systems. That's because they may silently communicate trust and expertise in a way the flashy extrovert never will.

Similarly, there are those who are quietly charismatic. We tend to think of the charismatic person as the one having so much star quality that he or she stands out like Rin Tin Tin at a cat show. But charisma, like sales skill, can be exercised in different ways. It doesn't necessarily mean being showy or flamboyant.

OUR OWN STYLES

Personal magnetism reveals itself very differently in different people. Each of us, as I've said, can develop it along the lines of our own personality, our own style.

I'm going to present five short statements made by people whom I've identified as persuasive. I'll let you decide if each one is something you might say about yourself.

No. 1: "I seem to have the ability to cut through the details and get to the meat, the things that count, the stuff that's going to impact the final outcome. I don't get bogged down. I don't let things that aren't related get in the way of making decisions or getting results."

No. 2: "I can get others to do things. I don't like the word *inspire*. It seems more like my enthusiasm and energy for getting things done makes people want to do them with me. They get excited about what I get excited about, and they want to do what needs doing."

No. 3: "I think people are attracted by my ability to size things up and solve a wide variety of problems. I enjoy coming up with solutions that nobody's ever tried before. I'm one of those people who wakes up in the middle of the night and says: 'Hey, I know a better way to do it.'"

No. 4: "I'm a natural listener. I find it easy to gather information, organize it, and then relate to the task and the people involved in the situation. I have a hard time when conflict exists. I like everyone to get along so I'm a peacemaker. I go in and smooth things out so we can get back to things running smooth and easy."

No. 5: "I love new information. I definitely turn a conversation or simply start a new one when I can relate something I've just read. I don't know whether other people will find it interesting, but most times they do. I mentioned something recently at a dinner party and another person picked up on it. Everyone joined in and the conversation went on for about twenty minutes. I was a real hit!"

Do any of those sound like you?

Those statements obviously came from a wide variety of people. Yet each of those persons can influence others positively in a different way. He or she may be forceful, or a good listener, or a results-oriented person, or a "people-person," or a high achiever, or a caring person, or some combination.

The point is that we all have an ability to influence people positively. But it may not manifest itself in some stereotypical way—like the fabled charisma of a certain great leader or the verve of some dashing celebrity. You possess unique strengths as an individual.

If you identify with *any* of the statements you've just read, keep that in mind! You now have a clue as to your special qualities. Meanwhile, we're going to build on that base. You'll be able to develop the skills you need to round out your approach and increase your ability to influence and persuade others.

NOT MYSTERIOUS

Because it sometimes seems so hard to nail down a definition, we often presume charisma to be a mysterious trait, something elusive, something difficult to study or learn. But it's not that mysterious—and, again, it's not an isolated gift as much as it is a cumulative combination of abilities and attitudes, which can be learned and practiced and parlayed, one upon the other.

Unfortunately, most people are brought up to think charisma is something that only others have, that it's something you either have or you don't—and, in either case, there's not much to be done about it.

But you can apply the seven keys, or elements, of charisma to your personal life, your job, or in any setting where the ability to influence others positively is beneficial. And—*ask yourself now!*—in what setting wouldn't that be beneficial? Unless you're a lone fur-trapper in the North Woods, or doing time in solitary at San Quentin, you're likely working and living with other people. Developing your charisma will give you the ability to draw those people to you—and the ability to give more back to them.

HARNESSING THE POWER

Recognizing charisma in its various forms is a first step toward harnessing its power. For example, you may have personally known actors or entertainers or media personalities who perhaps weren't all that impressive face-to-face but who could "turn on" when they took the stage or stepped in front of the cameras. That's a kind of contrived charisma, a veneerlike image that some people can use briefly and artfully to get a job done, whether it's attracting applause, impressing the boss, or getting a date.

Then there's another kind of charisma you may have noticed on occasion in yourself. You may have sensed sometimes that you're briefly a different, more buoyant, more spontaneous person. Swept up in the excitement of a situation, you feel exceptionally good about yourself for a time.

Maybe you've just gotten back from a marvelous vacation, or you've just nailed down a big promotion at work. Or perhaps you're in love, or are so passionate about an idea that when you explain it to the boss, you're so articulate you can hardly believe it's you who's speaking. Whichever the case, you walk around for hours, or even days, with an added bounce in your step and a smile on your face. And you ask yourself: Wouldn't it be great to be like this all the time?

Of course it would. But in both the contrived and the spontaneous situations, the charisma is kind of pasted on top of who you are. Instead, what we're aiming for in this book is genuine, sustained charisma, the kind that's a part of who you are, not just a temporary mask. I want to point you toward charisma that's deep and lasting.

People with that sustained charisma can maintain excitement about themselves that lasts beyond that initial, fleeting impact on others and beyond the giddiness of their own temporary joys. And the longer they maintain that deep excitement, the stronger it grows.

Again, it's not a single skill or trait, but a constellation of characteristics that, when honed, can help you to:

- Sharpen your ability to influence and motivate people by projecting confidence, energy, and a sincere interest in the goals and objectives of others.
- Connect with and empower people of all sorts by learning to listen to them, empathize with them, and support them.
- Become more positive by using the tools of positive thinking and surrounding yourself with optimistic people.
- Enhance your personal energy by improving your fitness, both physical and mental.
- Develop a powerful guiding vision for your life.

THE ORIGINS OF CHARISMA

The term *charisma* originated with the early Greeks and meant "a divine gift." The Christian Church later picked up the term to describe wisdom, prophecy, or healing, all attributes bestowed by God. In the early twentieth century, "charisma" became secularized by German sociologist Max Weber, who speculated that some exceptional figures had revolutionized politics by force of personality. He theorized that their charisma was "a gift that set them apart from ordinary men."

Other social scientists studied charisma in search of the ingredients of this charismatic personality. But when that proved a dead end, attention turned from personality characteristics to *behavior* as the source of charisma.

You can choose to practice, absorb, and master these behavioral skills. Anyone is capable of doing so. You needn't remain who you are. You can greatly improve your personal magnetism and be all you've always wanted to be: assured, commanding, stimulating, and energetic.

We're not born dull and boring. As small children, most of us are terribly expressive—*too* much so for our harried parents! But, little by little, we're taught to be fearful of sharing our real selves. "Don't touch!" we're told, or "Act adult now!" Then there's that ever-popular admonition: "Grow up!" which translates roughly as "Don't be spontaneous or fun loving."

Thus, we learn not to share our real selves with others. Whatever charisma we have tends to get buried beneath the expectations of others. Little by little, most of us learn to keep our feelings and emotions in check.

A SPECIAL SPARKLE

Yet, paradoxically, later in life, we react most strongly and positively to those who're open and spontaneous—those who don't fear rejection, who communicate a sincere interest in others, who stride self-confidently into the world around them. These are the people who have a special sparkle that makes us seek them out.

These are the people we say have "a great personality" or "are wonderful to be around." We're attracted to them because they're positive, because they have a vision, and because they have energy, expertise, and confidence that what they're saying and doing is right. It's not *what* they are—their title, the size of their bank account, or where they live. It's *who* they are—the special magic that surrounds them. It's that extra dimension, that special vividness they have that gives them a power and influence over others and thus, naturally, makes them successful.

Those successful people aren't just lucky. They're charismatic. And you can increase your ability to influence and motivate others, too, by developing your charisma. You need to begin with a very important assumption: *You do have these innate abilities—positiveness, energy, confidence, a sincere interest in others.* Those qualities are within you, waiting to be developed.

You can choose to study, absorb, practice, and master these skills. You can greatly improve your charisma and be all you've always wanted to be: assured, commanding, stimulating, and energetic. You can be a catalyst, not just one of the cattle.

UH-OH! YOUR FIRST TEST!

But before we start, here's a quick first assignment. Right now, off the top of your head: How would you rate your ability to influence others positively by connecting with them physically, emotionally, and intellectually? On a scale of 1 to 10, with 10 being tops, give yourself a rating.

My guess is you've probably rated yourself somewhere between a 4 and a 7. Am I right? If you gave yourself a 1, a 2, or a 3, your lack of self-esteem is dragging you down. Feeling better about yourself should become your first priority. If you gave yourself an 8 or higher, then you're already well on your way to being able to persuade and influence others.

ROLE MODELS ABOUND

The literature of business is loaded with leaders who've mastered the charismatic skills, whose personal magnetism has carried the day—sometimes even against enormous odds. Lee Iacocca, the savior of Chrysler, and Mary Kay Ash, whose cosmetics-marketing idea energized the nation's nascent female workforce, come quickly to mind.

But one of my favorites is the late Sam Walton, because he flew in the face of a lot of stereotypical business images. He didn't have an extra-fancy education. He shunned expensive suits. He didn't drive a big car ("What am I supposed to haul my dogs around in, a Rolls-Royce?" he asked), or make his face a staple of TV commercials.

25

But he did become what some have called the greatest entrepreneur of the twentieth century, with the possible exception of Henry Ford. Starting with a small five-and-dime store in Newport, Arkansas, Walton built the giant Wal-Mart discount chain and in so doing, became at one point the richest man in America.

He wove a strong emotional linkage with his staff and customers. He did so with cornball cheers, wacky wagers (once dancing the hula in a grass skirt on Wall Street to pay off a bet about profitability), seed-spitting contests, and in-house gospel groups, such as the Singing Truck Drivers. "We not only have a heck of a good time . . . we work better because of it," Walton wrote in his book, *Made in America*. "We build spirit and excitement. We capture the attention of our folks and keep them interested, simply because they never know what's coming next."

He not only created this strong emotional connection, he also had an overriding vision of discounting as a new trend that was going to sweep the country. Walton loved, absolutely *loved*, to find unusual items, price them as cheaply as possible, and then promote the dickens out of them in his Wal-Mart stores. Always a terrific promoter, he'd create an atmosphere of small-town fun—with bands, circuses, and donkey rides in the parking lot and mountains of detergent or underwear or minnow buckets in the store as well as greeters who'd say hello to each customer drawn in by the excitement and the low prices.

"It's almost embarrassing to admit this, but it's true," Walton wrote. "There hasn't been a day in my adult life when I haven't spent some time thinking about merchandising. . . . It has been an absolute passion of mine."

Even when Walton made a mistake—like the time he sent a huge shipment of Moon Pies, a gooey marshmallow snack popular in the Deep South, up to his

Wisconsin stores where they just sat there—he'd just shake it off and get on with his vision. Such passion and persuasion, plus enormous energy and a keen eye for talent and teamwork, allowed Walton to take a single, small variety store and transform it into the world's biggest retailer.

No one ever called him dashing or debonair. But his silent message was enormous enthusiasm. His persuasion and vision were legendary. He was an inspiring, if cornball, speaker, a good listener (rank-and-file employees were often stunned when the founder asked what *they* thought), and was a stickler for use of space and time (Saturday-morning management meetings, for example, were a keystone of the Wal-Mart culture).

For Sam Walton, then, many of the "glasses" of charisma runneth over. But despite great gifts, he never lost the common touch.

DEVELOPING THE POTENTIAL WITHIN YOU

But even if you or I never get a chance to head a corporation, spearhead a movement, or even hold office in the local PTA, we can use our charisma, present or future, to do good for ourselves and others, to make for positive change in ways large and small.

In other words, you needn't be superhuman. Whoever you are, wherever you are, you can increase your personal magnetism by developing the potential that's within you. But you must be sincere and hardworking. As we mentioned, at one time or another you've probably recognized the glowing ember of it within you.

Now the task will be to blow upon that ember until it's a flame, and then a blaze.

A WORD TO THE WISE

Before we move on, though, I want to sound a couple cautionary notes. Charisma, or personal magnetism, doesn't come overnight, and it's not a substitute for character or expertise. If you expect to influence others, you still must be good, very good, at what you do—whether it's flying airplanes, dispensing financial advice, mowing lawns, or designing software. And you must have a worthy goal larger than yourself.

Being charismatic is a marvelous advantage in any endeavor. But unless it's backed up by knowledge, character, skill, experience, and nobility of purpose, it will eventually be seen as the facade that it is. I'm sure you've known people who were charming but ineffective. Or who were slick but lacked the skill or inclination to work productively. Or whose enviable abilities were sometimes used for less than admirable ends.

The bedrock of all leadership is still performance. The leader isn't just the person who can command attention and fire up people. As I wrote a few pages earlier with the five statements by five different types of persuasive personalities, it's possible to inspire quietly, too, through technical ability as well as insight and honesty.

Furthermore, don't get hung up on the idea that to maximize your charisma is to achieve perfection, that being able to influence people is itself the goal of life. Personal magnetism comes in many flavors and can be used for good or ill.

And, in truth, charisma is a two-edged sword. Franklin Roosevelt, clearly both a charming and a charismatic man, could excite an audience hungry for reassurance—but so could the decidedly less charming Adolf Hitler or Charles Manson. Thus, charisma clearly can be used for good or evil, be it, say, by the Reverend Billy Graham, who's inspired millions, or the Reverend Jim Jones, who led hundreds of followers to mass suicide. At its best, charisma is a marvelously helpful tool in almost any endeavor.

But that's just what it is—a tool. And a tool must be used for the right purpose and in conjunction with our brains, our wisdom, our morals.

CHAPTER 2

◆

WHY CHARISMA IS MORE IMPORTANT THAN EVER

Perhaps you've heard of Steve Ross. He was an entertainment-industry legend who parlayed a small undertaking firm and a parking-lot business into the media conglomerate Time Warner. A flamboyant entrepreneur and the epic dealmaker of his generation, Ross died a few years ago, and, according to Connie Bruck's biography of Ross, he was eulogized thusly:

> Steve was a giant of a man—giant in his accomplishments, giant in his capacity for love, giant in his loyalty and concern toward others, giant in his energy, whether in business, on the tennis court, or on the dance floor, giant in his philanthropy and giant in his generosity of spirit. He gave more to every friendship than he took.
>
> He made all of us feel important and good. . . . He considered nothing impossible. He inspired us to perform beyond the limits of our abilities and made us better than we were. . . . There was a personal side to every

31

relationship with Steve. It was never all
business. He derived his authority from his
relationships, not his position.

That short description by a friend and mourner is
practically an item-by-item recitation of what we've
come to know as the cardinal points of charisma:
thinks big, thinks positive, thinks of others, and inspires
and motivates them to his larger goals.

All of Ross's charisma "glasses" seemed to be full, or
nearly so. But pay particular attention to the last sentence of that eulogy: "He derived his authority from his
relationships, not his position." That's important. And
it's what this chapter is all about.

THE ILLUSION OF POSITION POWER

We all can't be like Steve Ross—friend to glamorous
stars and maker of millions, spending our lives in the
center of a hurricane of important happenings. But we
can learn from such larger-than-life people. They show
us the awesome potential of charisma. And, further,
they show us that while charisma may sometimes lead
to the acquisition of titles or positions, ultimately, it is
who we are, not what we are, that counts. In fact, never
before have charisma and its by-product, personal
power, been more critical. That's because the gap has
widened between our ability to affect others by
"position power" as opposed to "personal power."

Position power is just what it sounds like: You're the
president, the pope, the head of the sales department,
the mother, the vice-principal, the coach, the guru, the
head nurse. The position itself confers some degree of

power. That power may stem from controlling resources (the budget, or, say, deciding who gets a corner office), from the ability to reward or punish people (a raise, a punitive transfer, or a pat on the back), or the right to wield certain prerogatives (such as signing contracts over a certain dollar amount or setting the rules for use of the company cars). The point is, no matter who has that position, he or she assumes the power that comes with the title.

EARNING A FOLLOWING

But ask any current CEO what happens if he tries to get the brand of ketchup changed in the employee cafeteria. Ask any vice-principal what happens when she tells a class of thirty junior-high students that they're staying after school if they litter the schoolyard. Ask any regional sales manager what happens when he asks the individual store managers to upgrade the signs in a uniform manner in all their windows.

"Leaders are almost never as much in charge as they are pictured to be, and followers never are as submissive as one might imagine," according to John Gardner, the founder of Common Cause and a former U.S. Secretary for Health, Education and Welfare. Leaders "can be given subordinates, but they cannot be given a following. A following must be earned."

So, more than ever in this age of individualism, sometimes bosses get their way—and sometimes they don't. With traditional authority carrying less and less clout, position power can have amazingly little impact in an institution, be it a family, business, school, hockey team, labor union, or what have you.

THE PHENOMENON OF PERSONAL POWER

So even if you have a title, you also need *personal power*. That's the kind of power that's freely given to the influencer from the people being influenced. And it's the kind that we heap more liberally on people possessing charisma.

While position power comes from *having authority over others*, personal power comes from *being respected and liked*. The truly charismatic person naturally has a leg up when it comes to amassing personal power, though of course position power and personal power work together terrifically. Combined, they can be a tremendous force.

A FLEETING KIND OF POWER

Position power can come from titles, occupations, affiliations, even clothes. But it's a fleeting kind of power. Titles are symbols of position power, and they suggest respect because they're usually difficult to acquire. We all have a different feeling if we're introduced to Barry Jones or Mary Smith, as opposed to being introduced to *Dr.* Barry Jones or *Judge* Mary Smith. Such titles project an image independent of the person who holds them.

There's a similar kind of position power implicit in some occupations, even if they don't carry a lofty title. Say you're asked your occupation by strangers at a cocktail party. If you say homicide detective, priest, lawyer, certified public accountant, television producer, or nuclear physicist, you send out a signal. All these jobs carry a mystique, and people in those professions gain some automatic position power without revealing another fact about themselves.

Being a recognized member of a prestigious organization can also confer position power. In some communities, being a member of the Junior League, the country club, the chamber of commerce, or the League of Women Voters, for example, automatically enhances your power.

In addition, we all know how uniforms carry authority. Dr. Robert Cialdini tells of an experiment by another psychologist in which a person, called a "requester," stopped pedestrians and pointed to a man standing by a parking meter fifty feet away. The requester always said the same thing to the pedestrian: "You see that guy over there by the meter? He's overparked but doesn't have any change. Give him a dime!" Then the requester turned the corner and was out of sight. But the power of his uniform lasted. When the requester wore a security-guard uniform, nearly all the pedestrians complied with his directive. Fewer than half complied when the requester was in normal street clothes.

So clothes can function like a title. They can give you authority. Uniforms, business suits, expensive jewelry, elegant purses or briefcases, even a ponderous-looking daily organizer can confer position power on you.

WHAT MAKES FOR PERSONAL POWER?

Personal power, though, can't come from titles or uniforms, from jewelry or belonging to the right clubs. Personal power is more like a magnet than a badge. It comes from within, from being the kind of person you are. And it's a key to making a difference with your life.

While jobs and status are fickle, *who you are* stays with you. And no matter what happens, if you have personal power, you'll always be able to handle change and difficulty more easily than the person who must rely on external symbols. Personal power will outlast position power every time.

In fact, think about some political or social leader you took a liking to. What was it about that person that first attracted you? I bet it wasn't primarily the title they held or the organization, if any, they commanded.

I bet it had something to do with a vision they articulated. They talked about a possible future that you found compelling. And they talked about it passionately and enthusiastically, infecting you with a sense of what could happen if you and others followed their direction. They had an image, or silent message, that appealed to you. They spoke well and confidently, listened to you, and adapted well to others. In other words, they probably had personal magnetism, or charisma. So, in short, trying to fill your "glasses" of charisma will pay big dividends because you'll develop more personal power in whatever role you find yourself.

WHY CHARISMA MATTERS NOW

The charismatic person, or leader (and the charismatic person is likely to become a leader, whether officially anointed or not), is a practitioner of personal power and, thus, a good match for our age. For starters, ours is an era of images. And, as we've seen, the person with charisma often exudes a strong, positive image, or

silent message. For better or worse, our society empha-
sizes the visual. So someone who makes a good first
impression, or perhaps is telegenic, has an immediate
advantage.

Second, I think our expectations have risen. We've
come to demand more from people than mere competence. When even the local car dealer or supermarket
manager can be seen as articulate, personable, and persuasive in a slick TV ad, we no longer readily accept
those who squirm, stumble over their words, and don't
quite look us in the eye. As a result, the able person with
a mind like a steel trap—but with an otherwise undis-
tinguished demeanor—is not as likely to impress us.

THE PERSONALITY OF A CINDER BLOCK

A hiring manager, for example, was faced with two perfectly qualified candidates for a quality-control (QC)
position. When she couldn't decide between them,
Dave Jensen, managing director of Search Masters
International, an executive search firm in the biotech
field, asked her why.

"I just can't bring myself to do it," she replied. "These
two QC managers have all the combined personality of
a cinder block." The manager, Jensen recalls, was
thinking, first, of how these two candidates would
interact with the public and, second, how they would
fare within the firm over the long term. The manager
said, "We need to hire people who can have an impact
both internally and externally." She added that if they
can't influence others positively, then they will always
be in the lab, largely isolated from the outside world and

unlikely candidates to succeed her. So, Jensen said, they started the search over "for a different sort of candidate."

So even science's reputation as a haven for nerds has changed. "When scientists and technicians hear the word *charisma*, they may first think of sales reps or politicians," Jensen says. "But you'd be hard pressed to find a person in any influential biotechnology position who doesn't have some measure of charisma."

CONNECTING WITH PEOPLE

A person who's developed his or her charisma is likely to do well in all aspects of life. Basically, that's because, on several different levels, they connect with people better. By definition, the charismatic person is more other-directed, more empathic. That gives them more personal power—and that's a big plus for anybody.

In fact, a recent survey by Cornell University's Johnson Graduate School of Management concluded that compassion will be one of the most important characteristics of business leaders a decade from now. Only team-building was cited more often than compassion by executives of Fortune 1,000 companies surveyed by the school.

This people-connectedness increasingly serves charismatic people well in any number of ways. The following shows how.

Empowerment

A key concept in management circles now is "empowerment." This, in short, means expressing personal support for others by allowing them—encouraging them, actually—to grow. The traditional leader was fearful that giving subordinates a long leash would somehow diminish his authority.

But the "new" leader, in effect, says: The more power I have, the less I should need to use it. I'll build power by giving it away, creating a loyal cadre of competent people who will work well and long because they like and trust me, not because I'm forcing them to work. Thus, the charismatic person, with special skills of adaptability and persuasion, is especially qualified to empower others—and therefore, to succeed in today's marketplace.

"While other business leaders may use empowerment practices, I suspect that the charismatic leader does so to a greater degree and often more skillfully," writes management professor Jay Conger in his book *The Charismatic Leader*.

Communication

It's almost impossible to be effective in the workplace without being an effective communicator. It's been estimated, for example, that as much as 80 percent of a typical manager's day is spent communicating. If this is true, then it's logical that the best managers are likely the most effective communicators. How could it be otherwise?

As mentioned in Chapter 1, a charismatic person is necessarily a strong communicator, with well-developed speaking and listening skills. In fact, communication is probably the most important source of personal power.

Much of this book, you'll discover, is devoted to communication, including speaking skills, active listening, and understanding other personality styles so that you can, in fact, speak their language.

Openness to Change

Another reason charisma is so important now is that this is the age of change: start-ups, acquisitions, turn-arounds, mergers, de-mergers, new regulatory climates, and all other sorts of rapid, unpredictable changes, especially in business. What's more, because people change jobs more frequently now, those aspiring to power can't rely as much on seniority, familiarity with the culture, or even technical skills. They need personal power, and that, in turn, sometimes revolves in part around how much risk they're willing to assume.

Casey Cowell, for example, dropped out of college and, with two friends and $200, founded U.S. Robotics. This was a high-wire act without a net. But the trio had the idea of building a crude computer-networking device that, when attached to a telephone, would tap into a remote mainframe computer. Working out of Cowell's apartment, the trio hand-assembled the products—which came to be known as modems. "It's a testimonial to what can be accomplished if you don't know better," says Cowell, now CEO of the $1 billion firm. "If you don't know what the outcome will be but are confident, you can accomplish great things."

Change inevitably entails risk, and thus, risk is an unavoidable by-product of exercising influence. I believe that charismatic people generally lack a fear of risk; in fact they may relish such risk. Even if they don't succeed, their boldness often adds to their charisma.

Take basketball star Michael Jordan, certainly one of the most charismatic athletes of recent times. Despite being the most-heralded professional player of his era, he quit the hardwoods to play minor-league baseball for a time. He didn't make it to the big leagues, but he didn't strike out with his millions of fans, who may have thought his ill-starred tenure with the Birmingham Barons made him, if anything, more human.

Positiveness

Another reason charisma is more important than ever is that amid all this change and heightened competition, people with such personal magnetism are usually self-confident optimists. Positiveness is the fuel that causes them to persevere and the license that allows them to take risks.

There is little doubt that a positive outlook propels while a negative one imprisons. Many studies have shown this. For example, Martin Seligman, a University of Pennsylvania professor and one of the foremost students of optimism, surveyed representatives of a major life-insurance firm. He found that, among the long-term reps, those who confidently expected a good outcome sold 37 percent more insurance than those with negative attitudes. Similarly, among the new hires, the optimists sold 20 percent more.

Impressed by Seligman's study, the insurer hired 100 applicants who'd failed the standard industry entrance test but scored high on optimism. Those people sold 10 percent more than the average rep.

Further, research by Seligman and others has shown that hope is a better predictor of college success than SAT scores or high-school grades. That's apparently because tests like SAT measure talent, not the motivation to keep going in the face of difficulty.

In business, an outgrowth of a positive attitude is that excitement and a sense of excellence cascade through an organization as more people feel inspired. Subordinates "model" the charismatic leader's attitudes and actions, and the whole organization can be imbued with a winning spirit.

Ed McCracken, the respected, long-time CEO of Silicon Graphics, Inc., is a firm believer that managers don't control as much as they inspire. Thus, he encourages a sense of fluidity, perhaps even chaos, by keeping the high-tech firm flexible and informal.

"We have a rule here of no long-term planning," he says. Employees being considered for positions are asked, "Do you mind having your desk moved three times a year?"

Viewing almost all problems as solvable—focusing on *desired results* rather than *possible failures*—helps encourage people to step forward and convert fear into challenge. Later, we'll talk about some specific techniques that will help you develop an optimist's attitude.

THE USES OF PERSONAL POWER

Again, the truly charismatic person operates more through personal power than position power. When position power alone is used, people are not really being motivated—they're just being temporarily pushed. By influencing through personal power, though, you create sustained internal motivation.

As you seek to improve your charisma and personal power, remember that when people feel someone is *making* them do something, they're often frustrated and resentful—and as a result, they dig in their heels. The truly influential person, the charismatic person, strives to create feelings of collaboration and equality.

Charismatic people approach others interactively and try to give them a choice.

This is what our era requires, and it's why, in a nutshell, charisma is more valuable than ever. Use interactive techniques to help influence people positively, and you'll not only improve your charisma, you'll improve your professional situation, no matter what your career.

Testing this doesn't require a big, important issue. Everyday tasks will suffice. For example, saying "Copy this report" is a mild form of coercion from a position of power. But "Would you mind copying this report?" or "Do you have time to copy this report right now?" is using the idea of interaction.

You can't mandate efficiency or productivity by ordering your employees to "Be more productive!" or "Improve your efficiency!" But you *can* organize them into teams, for instance, or create suggestion systems that really work, and give people more information about the company's profits and losses.

In addition, recognize the other person's achievements, contributions, and particular skills. Catch someone doing something *right*! And celebrate those successes. Everyone wants to feel that they're on a winning team.

Be aggressively optimistic and willing to be the first to do something and to take the heat if it doesn't work out. Charismatic people have heard all the bromides about why you can't rock the corporate boat ("We've never done it that way before." "It's too radical a change." "You're right, but . . ."); they just pay less attention to them.

Instead, they relish a challenge, not just for themselves but for their followers, too, who wish to take risks and be allowed to make some mistakes. So if you give them some control over resources and some influence over how to do a task, you'll help them build self-confidence.

In fact, the charismatic person often good-naturedly challenges, prods, and pokes as he or she encourages others to stretch themselves. Again, take Michael Jordan. He's said to be, even in practice, the loudest, most demanding player on the court, goading the other Bulls to give their all. It's his way of being inspirational; he never stops competing, even when no one is keeping score.

The potential to be a charismatic leader is within you. And the payoff for doing so has never been higher.

PART II

◆

THE SEVEN KEYS TO BECOMING MORE CHARISMATIC

CHAPTER 3

◆

SENDING OUT YOUR BEST SILENT MESSAGE

"First impressions are lasting impressions."

"The first impression is the only impression that counts and the only one that lasts."

"You only have one chance to make a first impression."

I'm sure you've heard such sayings, probably starting at an early age. But I would take those a step further and say that you make a statement about yourself even before you open your mouth.

This is your "silent message," and it can include everything from your posture to your positiveness. In short, it's the way you carry yourself, physically, emotionally, and intellectually. Such quiet signals profoundly affect people's initial perception, or image, of you.

Of course, image isn't everything—but it *is* important. As you know by now, doing well in life doesn't hinge solely on merit and hard work. Image, especially when backed up by strong performance, is a powerful force. And a negative first impression—saying the wrong thing, wearing the wrong clothes, coming across as uncaring or inept—creates roadblocks that can cut off relationships before they get started.

The truth is, we each carry around a bundle of opinions about what we like or don't like in others. If you hear a stranger laughing uproariously at the other end of a room, you'll probably make a quick calculation about that person. Maybe it's positive, maybe it's negative. But you do judge how their behavior fits the situation—even though you don't know them, haven't spoken to them, and may not even know what's being discussed.

We're all influenced by images. Researchers in Texas, for example, had a thirty-one-year-old man break the law by crossing the street against the traffic light. When the jaywalker wore a freshly pressed suit and tie, $3\frac{1}{2}$ times as many people followed him across the intersection than did when he wore a work shirt and trousers. So an acceptable uniform—in this case, business attire—made such a good first impression that it encouraged people to trust a stranger even to the point of breaking the law.

A CRUCIAL FIRST STEP

If a person matches our sense of acceptability, he or she has a head start in influencing us positively. When we meet people we immediately like, we tend to put a positive spin—at least, initially—on everything they say or do. Some call this favorable first impression *presence*. Others liken it to *energy*, or *aura*. (The latter sounds too much like a halo for me to believe *I* have one, but some people prefer that word!)

The point is, whichever term you use, people with a presence, energy, or aura are able to maintain an excitement about themselves that starts with—but usually lasts far beyond—a favorable first impression. Thus, we admire them before we even know much about them.

Because they win our admiration so quickly and effortlessly, they possess an enormous advantage in establishing a bond with people. And building that bond, forging those relationships, is what helps give you charisma.

QUICK QUIZ: YOUR SILENT MESSAGE

I'm going to ask you to respond to a series of statements. Take your time. It's important that you be utterly honest. You're the only one who'll see the answers—and you're the one with the most to gain by assessing your strengths accurately.

Don't try to guess the "right" response. There is no right answer; only your answer. Thinking about the response is as important as the response itself. Reply to each statement to the best of your ability, even if you're not sure. Don't worry about consistency among your responses; the pairs of statements aren't necessarily mutually exclusive.

For each pair of statements below, distribute three points between the two alternatives (A and B), depending on how characteristic of you the statement is. Although some pairs of statements may seem equally true for you, assign more points

---

to the alternative that is more representative of your behavior most of the time.

Examples:

- If A is very characteristic of you and B is very uncharacteristic, write "3" next to A and "0" next to B.
- If A is more characteristic of you than B, write "2" next to A and "1" next to B.
- If B is very characteristic of you and A is very uncharacteristic, write "3" next to B and "0" next to A.

. . . and so on.

1A___I usually have enormous physical energy and feel my regular program of physical fitness enhances what I do.

1B___Though I make efforts at keeping fit, I don't always stick to the program and so sometimes feel tired or run-down.

2A___I seldom say anything I regret.

2B___I find myself sometimes apologizing for outbursts and things I wish I hadn't said.

3A___When others follow my instructions, they do so because my approach was nonthreatening and helped them understand the value to them and to the organization.

3B___When others follow my instructions, they do so because they are more concerned about how I will evaluate them rather than because they think the task is necessarily the right thing to do.

4A___I almost always view a new project as an exciting challenge.

4B___I sometimes face a new project with thoughts such as: "I could never . . ." Or, "I'm terrible at . . ."

5A___I am able to discuss my accomplishments and my shortcomings honestly as well as to give and receive compliments readily.

5B___I sometimes get a bit defensive about criticism and, being essentially modest, I am also sometimes uncomfortable even with compliments.

6A___People comment that, for my age, I look pretty good. And they often comment on my smile, too.

6B___People rarely comment on my appearance or smile.

7A___When I ask a person with less authority (e.g., maid, child, employee, bank teller, grocery bagger) to do something, I almost always say "please" or am otherwise courteous to them.

7B___When I ask such a person to do something, I expect him or her to do the job, or fulfill the role, without much coaxing, just as I would do if I were in their shoes.

8A___I like the give-and-take of meeting people outside my normal range of experience. So I rarely feel out of place at a party of strangers.

8B___I often have difficulty carrying on a conversation with someone who works in a different field or lives in a distant city or has hobbies or interests different from mine. Thus, I'm often uncomfortable at parties with strangers.

9A___When I speak to someone who may have acted improperly, I tend to ask questions of him or her before stating my views.

9B___When I speak to someone who may have acted improperly, I believe in being honest by first stating my view of the behavior, then listening to his or her explanation, if any.

10A___I read at least one newspaper daily, subscribe to a

news magazine, and otherwise try to keep abreast of current events.

10B___My busy schedule precludes my keeping up with the news on any but an irregular basis, usually via local TV.

SCORING:

Please add point totals under "A" and enter here: _____

Please add point totals under "B" and enter here: _____

Now let's take a look at how you scored on this segment. If your "A" score is significantly greater than your "B" score, (and if you were truly honest!), you are fairly strong in this aspect of charisma. The more lopsided your "A" score, the stronger your silent message is. If your "A" score exceeds your "B" by, say, a 2-to-1 margin, your image "glass" is far fuller than most.

Conversely, if your "B" score approximates your "A" score, you may have identified an improvement opportunity. And if the "B" score is higher than your "A," that's an indication that you need lots of work in this area.

YOUR RAINBOW SELF

Maybe it'll help to think about your silent message this way: Imagine an invisible rainbow surrounding you. The "colors" of this energy rainbow are the different aspects of who you are. There are five hues in this particular rainbow, some brighter than others.

There is your *emotional* self, your *psychological* self, your *intellectual* self, your *spiritual* self, and your *physical* self. Together, they comprise the silent message you send out to the world. I'll be talking about each of these and, at the end of the chapter, suggesting ways you can jump-start your silent message.

In nature, some rainbows, of course, show off certain colors more than others. It's the same with people. They emit different kinds of energy to differing degrees. But I think we'd all agree that the best rainbows, whether natural or personal, are the ones where you can see as many colors as possible and in as vibrant hues as possible.

Emotional

Emotional energy has many components, but, for our purposes, the most important are a *positive attitude*, *enthusiasm*, and *self-control*.

THE POWER OF THE POSITIVE

Our mental attitude colors and shapes reality for us. Colin Powell, the son of Jamaican immigrants, rose from the streets of the Bronx to become chairman of the Joint Chiefs of Staff and one of the most admired men in America. In his best-selling book, *An American Journey*, he gives thirteen "rules" he's come to live by. Many of them embody the basic value of optimism, including:

It ain't as bad as you think. It will look better in the morning.

It can be done!

Don't let adverse facts stand in the way of a good decision.

Don't take counsel of your fears or naysayers.

Perpetual optimism is a force multiplier.

Optimists like Powell generally believe that power or control comes from within them. They feel they're ultimately responsible for their own successes. They view most problems as solvable, and thus, are willing to assume risks that might deter more fearful people.

Question: Would you rather invest money in a project with an 80 percent chance of success or in one with a 20 percent likelihood of failure? In one study, participants were asked that exact question. Without exception, they picked the former statement, though, of course, the two descriptions reflect exactly the same degree of risk. But aggressively optimistic people convert fear into challenge.

Do you tend to see a cloud behind every silver lining? If so, you're missing out on a lot of things, and probably the best you can hope for is to remain stuck where you are.

In truth, it's an immutable principle of life that whatever we focus on multiplies. Think gloom; you'll find gloominess all around. But think positively, and you'll be surrounded by opportunities.

We're not slaves to circumstance, but free to interpret life in our own way. Academy Award–winning actress Geena Davis, for example, left a New England mill town to pursue a film career in New York. Not able to find any movie jobs, she tried modeling. Not able to find any modeling jobs, she supported herself as a waitress, then as a department-store salesgirl. Repeatedly she was told she was too old (at age twenty-three) to succeed at modeling.

But she persisted, and eventually director Sidney Pollack saw her in a Victoria's Secret catalog and gave her a small movie role. "When I think about it now," she said, "it almost seems like naïveté, this unshakable blind faith that this was supposed to happen to me. I never considered giving up and going home. I always thought, 'Oh, it's just around the corner.'"

The Elixir of Enthusiasm

You generally wear your positiveness "inside." But your enthusiasm is how you show it to the world by your face, your voice, and your gestures. Sometimes we *feel* enthusiastic about our ideas but we're afraid to show it. But I think the people who influence us the most are those who are able to express on the outside what they're feeling on the inside.

A friend of mine remembers touring a client's office and seeing "cute" signs with negative messages plastered everywhere: "It's hard to soar like an eagle when you're surrounded by turkeys," "Even a bad day on vacation is better than a good day at work," and the like. Every message that every employee saw every day was negative. No wonder, my friend later concluded, morale there was so low.

Most people like to be around those who radiate joy and interest, whether at work or at play. What's more, enthusiasm is infectious. It spreads. But so does the lack of it. The choice is yours.

We've probably all worked with people who were negative about the job, the firm, their colleagues, the environment, the world itself, and then were further upset when—surprise!—they didn't get the big promotion. They chose to be problems, not problem-solvers. So was it any wonder that the boss would pick someone who was more positive and enthusiastic?

The response you receive from the world is in large

measure a reflection of your own attitude. From the beginning to the end of every meeting with another person, you are on stage: You're being evaluated by that other person, consciously or subconsciously. While I'm not suggesting you put on a phony happy-face, I am reminding you to be aware that your every word, gesture, expression, and impression is being watched—especially in initial encounters—and will either help or hinder you in fostering honest, open, and trusting communications.

If your overall approach is cheerful, hopeful, and tolerant of differences, you send out a positive message. On the other hand, if you're critical, pessimistic, and intolerant of anything unfamiliar, you convey a negative outlook. Guess which attitude gets better results when you're trying to influence people?

An Almost-Mesmerizing Bond

No one ever used the principle of positiveness more effectively than Franklin D. Roosevelt. An adult polio victim, Roosevelt would neither accept pity nor allow others to feel discomfort for him. Instead, recounts historian Garry Wills, the president, even while painfully "walking" by shifting his weight on locked braces, "would be smiling, keeping up pleasant banter, pretending to enjoy himself. It was an excruciating ordeal turned into a pleasant stroll." And if he fell, he got even more ebullient, despite the fact that it could take several strong men to raise him to his feet again.

His flow of jokes and chatter disguised his own suffering, which, some say, gave him an empathy with Depression-battered, then war-weary Americans. Before the crippling disease struck him at age thirty-nine, Roosevelt had been a child of privilege and was considered something of a political lightweight. But after polio withered his legs, he decided not to let the handicap get him down—and in so doing, he built an almost mesmerizing bond with vast segments of the American people.

FOSTERING "PAUSITIVENESS"

For a sustained good image, you also must master emotional self-control. "Those who command themselves," goes an old saying, "command others." That's true, and it means being disciplined enough to put your personal feelings on hold even when tempted to blow your stack.

If you otherwise make a great first impression, yet allow yourself to be pushed over the edge, to rant and rave, and to say and do things that you later regret, *that's* the "you" that will be remembered. Your hard-won image of positiveness or enthusiasm can be shattered in an instant. It will take a lot of damage control to undo even one such outburst.

One executive, whom I'll call Harry, seeks in normal times to project himself as fair, sensitive, highly knowledgeable, a good listener, and, above all, tranquil under fire. But his volcanic temper is never far from exploding. And when it does erupt in an outpouring of vitriol, no one is safe. And, later, no one looks him squarely in the eye for quite some time as he tries to resume his role as good ol' Harry, the wise, imperturbable leader.

What Harry needs is what I call "pausitiveness": the ability to pause and refrain from giving immediate feedback. Many an argument can be avoided if one side refuses to be defensive. That's because feedback, while generally a good idea, can be like throwing gasoline on a fire if you misunderstand the intent of the other person's message.

Another example: I once was at the home of some friends and was chatting with the wife when her husband, who was running a little late, burst into the room in an apparent huff. Pointing at his shirt collar, he demanded loudly, harshly, "Where did you get this shirt cleaned?" Many spouses, fearing a rebuke, might have counterattacked. But this woman, in a calm voice without disturbing body language, just named the dry cleaner and said evenly, "Why do you ask?" The husband said it was the first time any cleaner had done his shirt properly and he'd like all his shirts done there from now on.

So, clearly, there are times when it's best just to pause, bite your tongue, and restrain your body language and gestures in the face of an implied threat or criticism until the smoke has cleared. Maybe, as it sometimes turns out, there is no crisis at all, or perhaps you wrongly inferred that the other person was being critical. In any event, by remaining calm you may defuse the situation and, at the very worst, you won't aggravate it.

Remember: People will always believe that what you say in your worst moments is closer to your true beliefs than what you more carefully tailor for their consumption in calmer times.

Psychological

Another aspect of your image rainbow is your psychological self. There's a big overlap between the emotional and the psychological. But, for our purposes, the emotional is how you *feel* about yourself and your goals, and the psychological is how you *think* about them. Do you think of your goals as achievable? Do you think of yourself as a can-do person?

It's pretty easy to see that how you think about yourself directly affects your ability to exercise charisma. Not long ago, self-esteem expert and motivational speaker Jack Canfield co-edited (with Mark Victor Hansen) a book of inspirational stories called *Chicken Soup for the Soul*. Thirty publishers turned it down, and his agent gave up.

Yet Canfield persisted, walking from booth to booth at the American Booksellers Association convention and repeatedly receiving a thumbs-down. "The secret to persevering is building your self-esteem so you can take rejection and move on to the next opportunity," he says. "Self-esteem is critical. I'm living proof of the idea's validity."

Indeed, he finally found a publisher. And Canfield had been correct all along—it was a book America wanted. *Chicken Soup for the Soul* sold 1.5 million copies in its first 18 months. Almost overnight, Canfield went from owing almost $50,000 on his credit card to grossing more than $1 million from the book he'd been told wouldn't sell.

ACCENTUATING THE POSITIVE

It's been estimated that we each have upwards of 50,000 thoughts per day. How many of yours are negative? Sometimes you have to do a mental spring cleaning to get rid of those negative ones that have become ingrained attitudes. Stopping self-destructive thoughts is like stopping any other bad habit—it takes time and effort.

Among the most effective ways to do this are visualization and affirmations. Affirmations are positive statements about yourself that you repeat over and over in your head until they're programmed into your subconscious. Visualization, or "imagineering" as Walt Disney called it, is mentally picturing yourself the way you want to be.

You've heard the old saying "I'll believe it when I see it"? Well, the reverse is also true: "I'll see it when I believe it!" Affirmations and visualizations may not *feel* true at first. They may not even *be* true! But they can become so.

Consider what happens when you tell yourself over and over, "I'm lousy at remembering names." There will never be any improvement there. So if you catch yourself saying, "I'm terrible at remembering names," stop and immediately say to yourself, "I'm good at remembering names."

Or consider the effect of telling yourself, "I'm feeling pretty good today." Or "I *can* lose ten pounds." Or "I *am* good at getting people to see things my way." Anything you say to yourself over and over will actually influence your reality.

Writing down your affirmations in some handy place—above your desk, on your bathroom mirror, on the dashboard of your car—will help keep them in mind as well as in sight. Use affirmations and visualizations to project what success will feel like and look like. Imagine, in as much detail as you possibly can, how you feel as the boss singles you out for exceeding your quota, or how the audience hangs on your every word during your speech, or how your confident presence causes heads to turn everywhere you go.

EVERYTHING TO GAIN

You have everything to gain by talking to yourself positively. Canfield, for example, said, "When we were writing the book, I was always telling people, 'We're writing a best-seller.' I was saying it before it happened." That's an affirmation.

But he did more than that. He also took a copy of the *New York Times* best-seller list and physically inserted the name of his book in an identical typeface, then framed the hoped-for list and hung it on the wall. He also imagined himself being interviewed about the book on *Donahue.*

Those are visualizations. And Canfield kept affirming and visualizing his success until it actually occurred. Lots of people know about affirmations, and even believe that they could work. But few make the effort to follow through with this method. There are many fine books and audio programs on how to develop a more positive psychological self. The tools are there when you need them.

Intellectual

The third aspect of your personal image comes from how well you've developed what's inside your skull. This is your intellectual self. I'm not talking about a high IQ or your ability to win at Trivial Pursuit. I'm referring to the depth and breadth of your knowledge, your *mental* fitness. Most of us were given plenty of basic intelligence. We alone decide whether we'll use it to capacity or let it get flabby or stiff from disuse.

Can your mind lift abstract concepts from *The Wall Street Journal*, or from the professional journal in your field? Can you grasp the intricacies of a problem explained by someone in a field completely different from your own?

Can you see an issue from a perspective that's 180 degrees from your own feelings? Can you entertain ideas that come from a different culture, or from people you don't like? Can you hang in there when it's going to take a lot of convincing to get people to see things your way, or when it's going to mean clearing seven committees *and* the CEO?

Training your mind to take on longer-term and more demanding tasks gives you the stamina you need when mental marathons come up. Other ways to strengthen your mind might include:

- Taking some classes in a subject you've always wondered about—say, art history, acting, or geology—but never studied.
- Learning to play a musical instrument. Or, if you prefer, learning to scuba dive.
- Committing to teaching yourself a new and difficult skill: celestial navigation perhaps, or gourmet cooking, or origami, or wine-making.
- Joining a foreign-affairs group or an investment club or a reading circle where new issues and speakers abound.
- Buying an expensive subscription to a weighty series of books or musical performances. Paying so much, you'll probably feel compelled to get your money's worth.
- Here's a real test of mental discipline: Listening to a daytime TV talk-show without making judgments about the intelligence of the participants!

Another intellect-strengthening exercise is to get in the habit of not assigning labels to people. When you're at a party and another guest is introduced to you as "a life-insurance salesperson," don't you, mentally at least, take a couple steps backward? Ditto, perhaps, for "IRS auditor," "debutante," "parole officer," or "yachtsman," depending on your mind-set.

Thus, the hidden assumptions of language can control your behavior. Your preconceived notions of accountants, say, as bland and boring, or of professors as tweedy and reserved probably does you and them a disservice and may prematurely kill off what could be a valuable relationship.

To maximize your charisma, attempt to get past the labels. Don't overlook, for instance, the opinions of a mere "clerk" while perhaps overvaluing those of a "consultant." It takes intellectual strength to avoid the trap of confusing the specific for the general. But if you can get into the habit of appreciating people's unique, human side and not judging them generically, you'll win their respect—and you may learn something, too.

SEEK DEPTH OF KNOWLEDGE

Contrary to the old saying, what you don't know *can* hurt you. And depth of knowledge means, in short, how well you understand your area of expertise. The more you know about your subject, the more power and influence you'll have.

Let's say you're a salesperson, and one of the first sentences out of your mouth badly misstates the customer's situation. Instead of thinking "This person is sharp and can help me. I'd better listen up!", the customer will be wondering if you got your training via a correspondence course. He also may be busy figuring out how quickly he can ease you out the door and get a new account rep. In short, the depth of your knowledge wouldn't project credibility.

Charismatic people, on the other hand, often make good first impressions not because they're smarter than others but because they prepare better. When it's all said and done, some wit once noted, more is said than done. Acquiring depth of knowledge can help make you an exception to that cynical rule. And in some cases, it may even help overcome an initially bad impression.

For instance, a journalist named Dave was seeking a job in a foreign country, where he'd just moved. He made a bad first impression when, confronting a prospective employer, he nervously bobbled an easy question about the political history of his adopted nation. The publisher, who had been testing Dave for just such deficiencies, threw him out.

Dave spent the entire next day in the library undergoing a self-administered crash course in his new nation's history. Then he tracked down the same publisher, and before he could be ejected again, Dave disgorged tons of data about the nation's politics, past and present. He mentioned every politician of the last half-century, their parties, their triumphs, their defeats, their personal lives—everything!

The publisher, at first irritated to see Dave again, mellowed with admiration as he heard Dave recite his new knowledge. Impressed, he referred Dave to someone who did hire him, and Dave is now very successful in his overseas reporting career. Dave's depth of knowledge, though belated, saved his skin—and changed his life.

BREADTH OF KNOWLEDGE

If depth of knowledge alone were enough to make a good impression, chemists would have good initial rapport with other chemists, cops with other cops, and taxidermists with other taxidermists. But what about the rest of the world?

Breadth of knowledge is what enables you to engage

in meaningful small talk, and small talk, as O. Henry once said, is akin to putting "a few raisins into the tasteless dough of existence." In short, there's nothing small about small talk; it's a social lubricant that looms large in all human exchanges.

Thus, being informed on a wide range of topics outside your area of expertise can be immensely helpful in building social bridges. Research has shown that the more people feel they have in common, the better they like each other. So by increasing your breadth of knowledge, you'll be able to project a favorable image more easily with more people.

A young navy officer, recently engaged to be married, was taken to meet some relatives of the bride-to-be. They were the first of her large, impressive family he would meet, and he was understandably nervous. Imagine his surprise when the patriarch of the clan, a college president, said hello and then asked a series of informed questions about naval weaponry. Suddenly, the social distance and apprehension shrank as the young lieutenant was immersed in a stimulating conversation with a civilian stranger who knew, actually *knew*, something about naval ordnance.

The lieutenant never forgot how comfortable the older man had made him feel. And he never learned how a college president came to know so much about the relative muzzle velocity and rounds-per-minute of three-inch guns versus five-inch guns. Whether the older man was just uncommonly well versed or made a special effort to seek information that would put the young officer at ease, the fact remains that he built instant, lasting rapport.

How do you increase your breadth of knowledge? You're literally surrounded by opportunities! If there's one thing we don't lack in our culture, it's access to information. You can read books and magazines.

Explore the Internet. Take classes. Go to plays and movies. Attend workshops. You name it! All of these things—reading, doing, watching, listening—will increase your ability to build a bond with others and, thus, increase your charisma.

Spiritual

Your spiritual self, the fourth aspect of your charisma rainbow, has nothing to do with how often you go to church. Instead, by "spiritual," I mean the dynamic between you and those you're seeking to influence positively: the bond of trust you're able to create, the level of caring and the attitude of service you convey, and the sense of higher purpose or greater good that you communicate. It's sort of the opposite of self-centeredness.

I was struck not long ago by the tributes that followed the death of industrialist David Packard. He was, of course, eulogized as a can-do genius who, starting with $538 in cash and an empty Palo Alto garage, built Hewlett-Packard into a $31 billion firm and, after IBM, the second-largest computer maker in America. He was widely cited as "one of the most influential figures" in U.S. business history.

But amid the stories of his savvy management and progressive thinking, there were many anecdotes about David Packard, the man. An enemy of pomposity and immodesty, he was remembered for his generosity, his friendliness, his attentiveness to and trust in his employees (who called him Dave). He was as strongly devoted to people, many said, as he was to technology and sound business practices.

One friend remembered almost twenty years earlier when he was a middle manager preparing to give an important talk and, by chance, he met Packard in the parking lot. Packard asked him if he was prepared for his speech. The young manager said yes, but admitted he was very nervous. Packard, one of the richest, most powerful men in America, draped an arm around the manager's shoulder and said that was only natural.

Then he suggested the manager might find it easier if during his talk he imagined he was having a heart-to-heart conversation with his best friend. "Here was this really human guy who had immediate empathy with my concerns," recalled the then-manager, who now heads another electronics firm.

LEADING BY EXAMPLE

Another executive remembered having given a seminar, and Packard, after saying good-bye to the dignitaries, came over and helped put away the folding chairs. "He was holding three in each hand and carrying them down into the basement. I stopped and thought, 'This is a man who leads by example.'"

In short, Packard never forgot that character and kindness never go out of style. His charisma, enormous by any calculation, was made greater still by his humanity. And in the final analysis, that, as well as his company and his philanthropy, is his legacy. In short, he *cared*. That's the essence of this spiritual dimension that influences people.

So, to be as charismatic as you can, to send out the best silent message you can, you need be alert to the emotional states of others. That takes a well-tuned antenna. But such sensitivity is a definite spur to your charisma as well as a sign of character and decency.

Physical

I have saved this piece of the rainbow puzzle for last because I haven't wanted to imply that all you need to succeed is to be a sharp-looking smooth talker. That's like saying the applicant with the best-looking résumé—professionally typeset on the fanciest paper—should always get the job. Obviously, it's the person behind the résumé—the experience, the accomplishments, the integrity—who should count most.

But ask yourself this: What if the résumé is badly crinkled or soup-stained, contains obvious misspellings or grammatical errors, or presents the job-seeker's credentials in a confusing, illogical way? Regardless of how stellar the education or brilliant the career, that applicant probably would be dead meat if he or she couldn't produce a résumé that didn't meet at least minimal standards of acceptability.

So it is with physical image. Few are going to be fooled over the long run by someone who merely has a nice wardrobe and a good sense of grooming, a pleasant smile and a firm handshake, a smattering of knowledge, enthusiasm, and sincerity. But failure to attain those could easily undercut all your other skills and virtues.

Physical First Impressions

"Clothes don't make the man or woman. They make the message about the man or woman," writes master motivator Frank Pacetta in his book *Don't Fire Them, Fire Them Up*. "The message may be accurate or absolutely misleading—but it's a message nonetheless. We're not so civilized or sophisticated that we don't notice the limp handshake, the shifty eyes, the unpolished shoes."

As I said, we all carry around with us a bundle of opinions about what we like and expect—and what we don't like or expect—about others' appearance. If that appearance is out of sync with our opinion, it will create "noise," or distractions, in the communication process, making it difficult for the other person to hear what you're saying because they're distracted by, say, your bad toupee or ill-matched clothes.

A purchasing agent once told me how he was approached by a salesman who, at first glance, appeared impeccable: nicely coiffed hair, well-tailored suit, stylish shoes, leather briefcase, expensive pen, the works. Then the salesman crossed his legs, revealing white socks.

The purchasing agent was so astonished at this incongruity that he totally lost track of anything the salesman said. And, of course, no sale was made. Whether the salesman had a skin condition that required that kind of socks or whether he just didn't know any better, I don't know. But the effect was to torpedo his physical first impression. He never got a chance to make a second one.

Easy to Change

Fortunately, visual image is one of the easiest things to change. I've experienced that firsthand. When I began my public-speaking career, I wore very conservative suits that made me look like a banker. But then I got some valuable advice from Bill Gove, the first president of the National Speakers Association and a legend in the speaking world. He said to me, "Tony, you're trying to present an image of someone you're not. You're trying to talk and look like someone you're not. You're trying to come across too polished and conservative.

Think about it: You're a New York Italian. You'll be much more successful if you find a style that's right for you."

I began to loosen up my speaking style, and I allowed some of the faster-paced New York banter to slip into my speeches. After I gained some confidence, I began to wear Italian double-breasted suits, and I felt more "like myself," more confident and more at ease. Now I feel that my clothes match my actions and reflect more of who I am. An added benefit: Audiences also reacted much more positively to the changes.

WHAT'S YOUR PROPER IMAGE?

More important than specific clothing tips from me or anyone else is that you think about what image you want to project, and how it fits in the culture of your organization or industry. For example, one corporation that had gone through a traumatic downsizing decided, as a morale booster, to designate Fridays as "dress-down" day. Employees were encouraged to create a relaxed, end-of-the-week atmosphere by wearing casual clothes.

But one manager, widely viewed as uptight and compulsive, came to work that first Friday in a brand-new western outfit: pressed jeans and a belt with a large, gleaming silver buckle, starched shirt with a new bandanna knotted at his throat, and expensive, highly polished boots that had never seen a scuff mark, let alone a horse. He looked like he'd just come from a casting call for the musical *Oklahoma!* Thus, his "casual" dress did little to moderate his image as an out-of-touch authoritarian who couldn't learn to relax even if he took lessons.

The point is, appearance counts, and you've got to

look the part if you want to be credible. There aren't hard-and-fast rules about what you should wear, but there are general guidelines. The key question is: Do my clothes reinforce or detract from the impression I want to make?

As author Marcia Grad wrote: "Our appearance is an advertisement to the world." President John F. Kennedy once reportedly spent fifteen minutes combing his hair before stepping off *Air Force One* to greet a welcoming crowd in Berlin. "It's not Jack Kennedy but the United States that's going to walk off this plane," he explained. So it is for us all—it's not just us that people see but also the statement we choose to make about ourselves.

LOOKING HEALTHY

I don't need to convince you that if you're physically fit, you're going to come across better to others. We're all attracted by healthy-looking people. That's one of the joys of watching the Olympics, isn't it?

There are shelves of books and dozens of experts in your community to point you in the right direction. What you'll find, over the intermediate to long term, is that as your body gets used to the greater demands of exercise, you'll look better and feel better. You'll have more energy. Your self-esteem and self-confidence will also likely improve.

In short, you'll be more full of life. People will notice the difference, and your renewed energy and aura will have a positive effect not only on you but on those around you.

Tomorrow: The First Day of the Rest of Your Diet

Obviously, what you eat also affects how you look. Again, there are lots of books and classes that can tell you more about nutrition than I can here. But I do have one piece of nutritional advice: Know thyself.

We're all different in how we respond to different foods. Pay attention to how your body reacts. For example, many people get hyper after eating chocolate. For me, it's just the reverse: I feel sluggish.

Similarly, some of my friends on the professional speaking circuit always abstain from a big meal before an important talk, fearing it will cause them to lose their edge. Me, I eat a full meal. Or exercise strenuously. Either way, I feel sharp. But if I starved myself or sat around doing nothing for hours before a speech, the results wouldn't be nearly as good.

In short, find out what works for you. Consider keeping a log of what you eat and how you feel afterwards. Then experiment with different foods at different times. You'll add to your energy and, thus, to your charisma.

Other Physical Signs

Besides clothes, fitness, and diet, other aspects of personal appearance can make or break first impressions. Your handshake, as Pacetta says, should be strong and firm. But be careful not to overdo its strength or duration.

A more subtle element is eye contact. Think for a moment about what a powerful force it is in our culture. We summon a taxi driver or a maître d' by "catching their eye." We flirt through eye contact. Or, by withholding eye contact, we signal others that we lack interest in, or even disbelieve, what they're saying.

Thus, eye contact can be a potent tool for building a bond, or for damaging one. So if you're shy, or if you process information more through sound and touch than through sight, you may forget to look the other person straight in the eyes. Yet eye contact is vital—and not just the first time you say hello, but all through the conversation.

Posture is important, too. Influential people convey confidence and enthusiasm by carrying themselves, as Grad writes, "proudly but not pompously." This means standing tall with head and shoulders back, but with muscles relaxed. If you've spent years with your shoulders rounded forward or your weight on one hip, it'll take some practice to straighten yourself out. But it's worth it. Not only do you look better if your posture is good, you feel better, too.

SHORTEST DISTANCE BETWEEN TWO PEOPLE

The final element of a good physical first impression is a smile. Again, like eye contact, a smile is a small gesture with a powerful impact. In American culture, we've come to expect likable, approachable people to smile when we meet them.

Pianist/comedian Victor Borge put it another way when he described a smile as "the shortest distance between two people." Greeting someone with a warm smile is the best way to introduce yourself, and it sets the stage beautifully for any discussion that follows.

But many people think they're smiling when they're barely parting their lips. Check your smile in the mirror. As you step toward it, before you see yourself, put on your best smile. Then look at yourself. Is this person smiling or smirking? Is it really a happy smile or a forced smile? And are your eyes smiling? That's the test of a real smile.

If only your lips move, it's not much of a smile. Watch celebrities, politicians, or the hosts on late-night talk shows. The gesture may or may not be genuine, but these people definitely know how to smile.

JUMP-STARTING YOUR WAY TO A BETTER IMAGE

Here are some other ideas on projecting a positive image:

1. *A winning image starts with a good self-image.* A good self-image doesn't follow success—it precedes it, as Robert L. Shook says in his book *Winning Images.* Someone saddled with a poor self-image may fool some people some of the time, but eventually he'll fail, unless he comes to grips with his basic self-image.

In her best-selling book, *The Revolution Within,* feminist Gloria Steinem said she was shocked when she first saw herself on television. What she saw was a thin, pretty, blondish woman of medium height who spoke in a boring, though confident, monotone. But what she felt like *inside* as she was doing the interview was a plump brunette from Toledo who was too tall, much too pudding-faced, and cursed with a voice that was constantly on the verge of some unacceptable emotion.

Many of us carry around an image that doesn't really jibe with the facts. You could be holding a negative self-image, like Steinem did, that you subtly communicate to everyone you meet. If you feel that you're too tall, or overweight, or unattractive in some way, you'll lack confidence, and others will catch on.

Or it's possible you could have an overly positive image of yourself. You may think you look terrific, when in fact you're a sloppy dresser who's twenty pounds overweight and badly in need of a haircut or a makeover.

In either case, analysis by yourself—and perhaps by those closest to you—is needed because, as I've sought to show in this chapter, your image *is* important, and you *can* do something about it! To find out how others see you, get some photographs or videotapes taken of yourself when you feel you're looking your best. Specify close-ups and then study them carefully. What do you see that you like, or don't like?

Then ask your best friends for their candid opinions on not only how you look, but how you carry yourself, how you come across verbally, and what your car or house or briefcase or other material goods say about you. Promise you won't take offense—and don't!—then ask them to tell you also about your image in terms of knowledge and enthusiasm as well as sincerity and integrity.

2. *Make your wardrobe work for you.* Often we acquire our clothes haphazardly—a sale item or an impulse buy here, a Christmas gift there—without much thought as to how they fit our image, or even if they match each other. In fact, you've probably seen folks who've expanded their wardrobe only to hobble themselves by wearing a plaid shirt with a striped tie, or to go overboard with jewelry that clatters and clangs when they walk. In other words, unless you know how to put it all together, you can improve your wardrobe but still project a poor image. So make sure your colors, patterns, and accessories are complementary, not clashing.

Most of us have at least one or two outfits that make us feel especially good when we're wearing them. We tend to save those for special occasions. But why not try to increase that number to three, four, or more such outfits and, thus, try to make a particularly good impression every day?

If you're vague about what you look best in, consult a friend or co-worker whose taste you admire, or go to a wardrobe consultant. They often spot things that you'd look good in but probably wouldn't consider trying on.

A wardrobe consultant may sound like a costly luxury. But many times their advice is free if you buy clothes from them, and some will even shop for you at an hourly rate, which can save a lot of time. Combine that time savings with greater selection and the likelihood of a superb fit, and it all may add up to a terrific value.

3. *For maximum effect, freshen up.* Men should consider carrying a portable razor and a small stash of toiletries to ward off the worn-out, end-of-a-tough-day look before a business meeting in the late afternoon or early evening. Similarly, women probably should have cosmetics and hair-care items handy and maybe even an extra pair of earrings or other fashion accessories to give their appearance—and maybe their spirit—a boost.

4. *Avoid annoying or distracting habits or mannerisms.* Rarely do impressive people cover their mouths or noses, scratch their heads, chew on a pencil, twist rubber bands around their fingers, or tear their napkins into shreds while talking. Marcia Grad calls these habits "charisma robbers" and includes among them:

- Tugging at clothing
- Drumming fingers on a table

- Tapping pencils or clicking pens
- Doodling
- Jangling keys or change
- Biting nails
- Cleaning teeth

Not only do these habits make it more difficult for the other person to hear you, they also detract from your image.

5. *Go first-class on professional tools.* Don't scrimp on image enhancers like business cards, letterheads, pens, and briefcases. Getting quality stationery and accessories will cost only a few pennies more in the long run while making you look—and feel—more professional.

6. *Seek winners, spurn losers.* Attitudes are contagious! So nurture your emotional well-being by choosing friends who genuinely want you to succeed and who encourage you. Also, ask yourself about your surroundings: How's my house or apartment decorated? What about my office? Is it drab, or energizing?

Read some inspirational and motivational books. Or listen to happy music. (Have you ever heard a mournful banjo tune?) Or make it a point to go to funny movies or watch a TV sitcom that makes you laugh.

Consciously reduce your exposure to the negative, whether it's gossip from co-workers, violence in the media, or pessimism in your own thoughts.

7. *Practice treating everyone—from the janitor on up—as if he or she is the most important person you'll meet that day.* This will mean seeking to replace arrogance with empathy—not an easy task for a lot of people. However, it's a real test of character, and every

once in a while, you'll learn a big lesson from that "little" person.

In *The Seven Habits of Highly Effective People*, Stephen Covey repeats a wonderful story about a captain who spied a light coming through the fog toward his battleship. The captain ordered a signal sent by flashing light: "We are on a collision course, advise you change course 20 degrees."

Back came the signal: "Advisable for you to change course 20 degrees."

The captain messaged back: "I'm a captain. You had better change course 20 degrees."

"I'm a seaman second class," came the reply. "You had better change course 20 degrees."

Now furious, the captain spat out the message: "I'm a battleship. Change course 20 degrees."

Back came the flashing light: "I'm a lighthouse." The captain changed course.

8. *Give sincere compliments.* Sometimes people don't tell themselves—or maybe don't fully believe it—when they do a good job. So they'll appreciate you mentioning it.

Even the most hardened person, despite saying otherwise, *does* care what others think. "I can live for months on a good compliment," said Mark Twain, who was as accomplished a writer and wit as any man of his day.

9. *Don't just say it, do it!* Words, while important, are cheap. Credibility is gained by backing up those words with action. Especially if you're in a leadership position, be very aware that you set the style, both in appearance and integrity. Cultivate a do-as-I-do, not a do-as-I-say, philosophy.

You can show your sincerity by practicing what you preach on a daily basis. One manager, for instance, demanded his subordinates be pillars of strength when it came to refusing gifts from clients who might then expect special treatment. A day of reckoning came when the manager, known for his insatiable sweet tooth, received a gift of two chocolate pies from a local pastry shop. It's said there was a tear in his eye—and probably a pang in his stomach—as he had the pies returned with a gracious note. Everyone in the office had been watching—and he *knew* it—to see if he would be true to his own credo.

10. *Make fitness a lifestyle, not a chore.* You don't need an expensive club membership or a cross-country ski machine to maintain a body that exudes vitality. Forget the spandex, stopwatches, and ankle warmers, for instance, and just:

- Walk up and down the stairs to your high-rise office or apartment.
- Ride a bike to the neighborhood convenience store to pick up that quart of nonfat milk.
- Skip the cart and get some real exercise while golfing.
- Take a nature hike instead of watching a nature film on television.
- Got a friend you meet with regularly to shoot the breeze? Get in your chat while walking around the neighborhood instead of over a cup of coffee or a beer. You'll both be better off.

CHAPTER 4

---◆---

SPEAKING WITH AUTHORITY

When Arkansas governor Bill Clinton, in his nominating speech for Michael Dukakis at the 1988 Democratic National Convention, spoke the words, "In closing . . . ," a roar went up in the convention hall. He was *finally* finishing!

Fortunately for him, his 1992 speech, accepting his own nomination, got much better marks. In fact, some said it was the best speech of his life. Not only was it important as a kickoff for his first presidential campaign, but Clinton erased once and for all the memory of that dud four years earlier.

That story has at least three important points. One, you're never too good or too experienced to ignore some of the fundamentals of good speaking. Two, you can give an occasional poor speech and still retain your charisma, as Clinton did in the intervening four years. And three—and most important—the ability to communicate well to groups of people can make a critical difference in your career.

In fact, a study conducted by AT&T and Stanford University revealed that the top predictor of professional success and upward mobility is how much you enjoy and how good you are at public speaking. Yet surveys also show that the number one fear of most adults (even above death) is speaking in public.

Now there's a contradiction for you: The best thing for anyone's career is also what we most fear! In this chapter, I'm going to try to put that fear to rest.

Because, in truth, the ability to speak confidently is not only one of the major underpinnings of charisma, it's also one of the most marketable skills you can acquire. Organizations continually seek individuals who can sell products, present proposals, report findings, and explain ideas effectively. It's no coincidence that more than 50 percent of Toastmasters clubs are in-house corporate or government groups.

Audiences, accustomed now to slick media, are less tolerant than ever of marginal presentation skills. So the ante has been upped, the bar has been raised, on what level of public speaking is now needed to get your message across.

WHAT IS PUBLIC SPEAKING?

Actually, almost all of our speaking is public speaking— it's just the size of the audience that changes. (Audience size, in fact, can be overrated. Winston Churchill, one of the twentieth century's greatest orators, claimed not to be impressed that 10,000 people would gather to hear him speak. "Ten times as many would come to see me hanged," he quipped.)

Public speaking can take many forms: giving a speech to a large audience in a public forum, presenting a proposal to a conference room full of board members, or addressing one other person in a formal environment, such as a sales presentation. If your presentation is boring or unprofessional, it can leave you with nothing but a weak round of applause, or cause you to lose the sale. Worse yet, it may lower your reputation in the community.

The road to the White House, for example, is littered with the carcasses of able men of both parties who had vision, experience, and expertise, but who mumbled, bumbled, and stumbled rhetorically. So speaking counts. It counts for a lot.

Good presentations can provide opportunities for growth, recognition, and prestige. Effective public speakers establish themselves as experts to whom others turn for advice. Thus, being able to stand on your feet confidently and express your thoughts clearly and logically is a major building block of charisma.

QUICK QUIZ: YOUR SPEAKING SKILLS

For each pair of statements below, distribute three points between the two alternatives (A and B), depending on how characteristic of you the statement is. Although some pairs of statements may seem equally true for you, assign more points to the alternative that is more representative of your behavior most of the time.

Examples:

- If A is very characteristic of you and B is very uncharacteristic, write "3" next to A and "0" next to B.

- If A is more characteristic of you than B, write "2" next to A and "1" next to B.

- If B is very characteristic of you and A is very uncharacteristic, write "3" next to B and "0" next to A.

. . . and so on.

1A___When I make a presentation, I often become more aware of the audience than I am of myself.

1B___When I make a presentation, I'm almost always intently focused on my words and my message rather than the audience.

2A___I am usually calm and collected before I give a talk.

2B___I commonly suffer stage fright before I give a talk and sometimes get a little annoyed at myself for being that way.

3A___I research my audience as well as my topic before giving a presentation.

3B___I consider myself a good talker who can often "wing" the subject matter and quickly adapt to almost any audience.

4A___People tell me my speeches are witty and enjoyable.

4B___People don't say a whole lot after my speeches, but I usually have the sense that my major points sank in.

5A___I always emphasize at the end of a speech what I want the audience to know or to do.

5B___I make my points clearly and concisely during the main body of my speech and pretty much let them stand for themselves.

6A___I make visual aids an integral part of my speech, working hard to make sure they present in an interesting way the right amount of information.

6B___My words are what count; visual aids are kind of a crutch.

7A___I rehearse my speech, but I don't commit it to memory.

7B___I'm less nervous if I know every word by heart.

8A___I know the one main idea I want to present.

8B___My speeches are full of ideas, many of equal importance.

9A___I try to involve the audience in my speech—asking them questions, encouraging group exercises, filling out brief questionnaires, and otherwise urging participation.

9B___I avoid gimmickry and concentrate on the matter at hand, conveying my words as clearly as possible.

10A___I look at each speech as an opportunity to present my ideas and a chance to improve my presentation skills.

10B___I see giving a speech as a part of my job, a necessary evil.

SCORING:

Please add point totals under "A" and enter here: _____

Please add point totals under "B" and enter here: _____

Now let's take a look at how you scored on this segment. If your "A" score is significantly greater than your "B" score (and if you were truly honest!), you are fairly strong in this aspect of charisma. The more lopsided your "A" score, the stronger you are as a public speaker. If your "A" score exceeds your "B" by, say, a 2-to-1 margin, your speaking "glass" is far fuller than most.

Conversely, if your "B" score approximates your "A" score, you may have identified an improvement opportunity. And if the "B" score is higher than your "A," that's an indication that you need lots of work in this area.

BUILDING YOUR PRESENTATION SKILLS

We've all sat through boring presentations by speakers who were scarcely qualified to lead a group in silent prayer, let alone give a talk. After what seemed like hours, we still didn't know what message we were supposed to get. Maybe the speaker put us to sleep with a monotone presentation. Or maybe we couldn't read the small print on the transparencies. Whatever the reason, the result was the same: a disinterested, unmotivated audience. (The late Catholic clergyman and educator Bishop Fulton J. Sheen once warned an audience: "When you applaud me at the start, that's faith; midway through, that's hope. But, ah, my dear friends, if you applaud me at the end, that will be charity!")

To avoid requiring such charity, you need to build your presentation skills. In this chapter, you'll learn some simple steps for overcoming stage fright and for preparing and giving a successful presentation. You'll also receive pointers on improving your vocal image as well as how to use the six nonverbal power communicators—your *eyes, face, hands, arms, legs,* and *posture*—to project positive emotions such as openness, readiness, enthusiasm, and thoughtfulness.

OVERCOMING STAGE FRIGHT

Almost every speaker, actor, musician, and performer at times experiences stage fright, often in the form of sweaty palms, quaking voice, and jellylike knees. If it happens to you, you'll likely avoid making eye contact or may engage in erratic pacing or rocking. When you do speak, it may be in a monotonous voice and with a blank facial expression. Such behavior is a tip that the speaker is overwhelmed with self-consciousness, that he or she has succumbed to what's called butterflies in the stomach.

While the fear never goes away entirely, professionals know, as Art Linkletter once said, that you can make the butterflies fly in formation. In other words, you can learn to manage your fear.

First, understand that stage fright is a very normal reaction. No one is immune. Demosthenes was the ancient Greeks' greatest orator. But when he gave his first public speech, he stammered so torturously and feebly that the audience laughed him out of the assembly.

As a result, Demosthenes practiced alone for weeks. He cured his stammer by speaking with pebbles in his mouth and overcame his shortness of breath by reciting poetry while running uphill. Eventually, he held Athenian audiences spellbound.

Cicero, the brilliant Roman orator, admitted, "I turn pale at the outset of a speech and quake in every limb and in all my soul." Stage fright even affected Churchill, who described his prespeech anxiety as feeling like a nine-inch block of ice in the pit of his stomach. And actress Katharine Hepburn is legendary for her extreme nervousness before she makes any live appearance. If speech anxiety can affect such famous and talented communicators, obviously it can plague anyone.

SEEKING POSITIVE ANXIETY

You can overcome stage fright by approaching it with the right attitude. The way you feel about yourself, the audience, and the subject—as well as how well you've prepared and how hard you've worked on delivery— will have a direct impact on you as you walk toward the podium. With a good attitude and effective preparation, you can convert a paralyzing fear into *positive* anxiety, which keeps you sharp.

Sometimes just admitting to yourself that you're feeling anxiety helps to relieve it. Remember, too, that the reason you're speaking is because you're the expert. Those who ask you to speak believe that you have something of value to share. And the people in the audience believe they'll receive information of value.

So your first duty is to find out what your audience needs to know, and then prepare and deliver your message clearly and powerfully. Make a strong, wholehearted commitment to your audience. Concentrating on them and their needs will help you forget about your self-consciousness.

Here are some other quick tips for overcoming stage fright:

- Know your material well. *Be* the expert.
- Then practice your presentation. Do a dry run and, if possible, videotape yourself.
- Establish rapport by using names or making references that people in the audience recognize. If possible, make friends with at least one person in the audience before you speak. As you're speaking, look directly at specific individuals in the audience.
- Always try to check in advance the place where you'll be speaking and the audiovisual equipment, if any.
- Make sure you're dressed appropriately for the audience. It's better to be slightly overdressed than underdressed.
- Use your own style. Don't try to imitate someone else.

And here's a final guideline that is absolutely indispensable: *Don't forget to breathe.* Much of the physical discomfort of stage fright is caused by lack of air. If you need to, put a small sign on the podium that says: BREATHE.

PREPARING THE TALK

"If I had eight hours to chop down a tree," Abraham Lincoln said, "I'd spend six sharpening my ax." Good point! What makes one presentation better than the next is the amount of time that goes into it *before* you assume center stage.

For example, Churchill's broadcasts to the English people and his speeches in the House of Commons during World War II are legendary. But they weren't necessarily spontaneous. In fact, one of his contemporaries complained, "Winston has devoted the best years of his life to preparing his impromptu speeches."

Planning the speech involves six steps:

1. Identifying the purpose of your presentation
2. Knowing your audience
3. Knowing your material
4. Focusing on the Big Idea
5. Getting and holding the audience's attention
6. Practicing your presentation and visualizing success.

1. What's the Purpose?

The first and most critical step in planning your speech is understanding the "what?" and "why?" of your presentation—its purpose. Surprisingly, many people overlook this step and end up lost. And if you, the speaker, don't know where you want to go, how can the audience possibly follow you? Here are three questions you can ask yourself to clarify your purpose:

- Why am I giving this talk?
- What do I want the audience to know or do at the end?
- How do I want the audience to feel?

Why do you want to gain influence with these people by giving this presentation? Is the purpose of your speech to propose an objective that everyone can share, such as "We should work to improve our corporate image" or "We need to approve the new marketing plan"? Those are *end* issues.

Means issues are those that already have an end proposed—such as improving the corporate image or adopting the marketing plan—but now you're trying to influence people about *how* to do that. So you're advocating a particular means to that end.

For example: "In order to improve our corporate image, we need to design an advertising campaign highlighting our philanthropy." "In order to increase our competitiveness, we need to spend more on research and development." As you begin preparation for your speech, you should figure out whether your focus is an end or a means, or both.

The second question for identifying your purpose is this: What do I want the audience to know or do? Some presentations aren't meant to persuade an audience;

they're just entertaining or instructional. But because the focus of this book is charisma, let's concentrate on presentations that seek to persuade. You need to know what you want the audience to be persuaded about. Remember that purpose could be an end, or a means to an already shared end.

Third, how do you want the audience to feel when you're done? They're inevitably going to have some feelings. Why not encourage emotions that reinforce what you want to promote? Do you want them to feel uplifted? Emotionally touched? Angry? More appreciative of who you are? Rarin' to go?

The more aware you are of the feelings you want to promote, the better you'll choose your words and images to elicit those emotions.

2. Who's Your Audience?

Will they be open to what you have to say? Hostile? To which of their needs should you pay most attention? What background and knowledge do they have about your topic? What negatives have they heard about this topic? Do they have the authority to make decisions about your proposal? What's in it for them if they listen to you? Are you speaking in the morning, when people's attention level is high? Or after dinner, when it's going to be tougher to hold their interest?

There's a rule of thumb for how much content-versus-entertainment value your talk needs, depending on the time of day. Before noon, the balance should be 75 percent content versus 25 percent entertainment if you hope to hold the audience's attention. From noon to six o'clock, the balance should be about 50-50. And at night it should be 25 percent content, 75 percent entertainment. So after-dinner speeches are the

Charisma

toughest. Try to avoid them unless you're a very humorous or entertaining speaker.

(Obviously, these percentages depend also on the situation. If your talk is to the board of directors about whether to fund a major project, you'll want to stick to the issues and go easy on the entertainment, regardless of the time of day.)

But how do you get all the answers you need to know about the nature of the audience? Ask the presentation host for information. If you don't know already, find out the general demographics of the audience, such as age, sex, professional level, specific interests and needs. Also ask what the group has responded well to in the past. If possible, talk in advance to members of the audience. Arrive early enough to survey one or more of them to find out what they expect and what they'd like to hear. And talk to other speakers who've spoken to the same group.

When I've been contacted to do a presentation, I have my office send out what I call my "PPQ"—Pre-Program Questionnaire. I ask about the theme and purpose of the meeting; the other speakers who are going to be there, an analysis of the audience, logistics of the meeting place; general background on the organization and the specific issues it's dealing with right now.

Also, I think it's important to ask about people's titles. You don't want to keep referring to sales reps when they're called "account executives" or employees if they're called "associates." For example, I found out when I spoke to a restaurant chain that the diners were always called "guests," not customers.

In addition, here's an important principle from the world of selling: Leave them with *something positive*. Even if you don't achieve the objective you have in mind, leave them with an important intangible—a new

92

piece of information, a good feeling about themselves, or at least a sense that you're a person of integrity. That leaves the door open for a future attempt at establishing influence with this group.

3. Do You Know Your Material?

If you're not sure what you're going to say, not sure of facts about your topic, unable to take questions from the audience, then, of course, you're going to be nervous. You *should* be!

Preparation allows your delivery to flow, and it puts your audience at ease. That's because your audience is at ease when you're at ease, and you're at ease when you know your material and *know* you know it.

4. Focusing on the Big Idea

Once you know your audience, you're clear about your purpose, and you're committed to thorough preparation, then you're ready to focus on the Big Idea of your material. This is the power punch, the one thing you want your audience to walk away with.

An important point: This Big Idea must be made relevant to your listeners. So emphasize what's in it for *them*, how and why they will be better off by knowing this information.

You'll need to structure your presentation so it supports your one Big Idea. Of course your message will contain more than one idea, but they should all reinforce the primary focus of your idea and its relevance to the audience.

For instance: "We need to support literacy efforts in our community because these young people are the people who will be working for *your* companies, answering *your* calls for service, and voting for *your* public officials. Do you care if these individuals can't read?"

Here's another scenario: "We need to actively support and integrate women and minorities into the senior management of our company. It's the key to operating in a global economy. We're developing trade partners in many different cultures, and minorities and women are a large part of the workforce in those countries. Developing diversity in this company will give us a real competitive advantage."

The one Big Idea in the first message, which can be stated or left implicit, is this: *You* are going to suffer if you let illiteracy go unchecked. Here's the Big Idea from the second scenario: In order to compete in a diverse world, *our* company must reflect that diversity. Similarly, if I were to summarize the one Big Idea of this book, it would be: Gaining charisma is not mysterious; *you* can learn it.

As you outline your presentation, limit yourself to no more than seven ideas that support your one Big Idea. And as you develop the details and images for your speech, keep checking back to your one Big Idea and make sure it all relates directly.

5. Getting and Keeping an Audience's Attention

There's an old saying among speakers: "Have a powerful, captivating opening and a strong, memorable close—and put them as close together as possible." Sad to say, many beginning speakers lose their audience right off the bat.

Instead, grab your listeners with something vitally interesting to them. In one of my frequent talks about improving relationships, for example, I start off by asking for a show of hands from those who've ever had a personality conflict. Naturally, almost everybody raises his or her hand—so right away I've got nearly everyone's attention because they realize they're about to learn something helpful.

Give them an exciting, interesting story or example that leads into your focus. Try to draw them into the subject by using a strong quotation or a startling statistic. Be succinct, and use simple, graphic language.

Most of all, never apologize! If the airline lost your bag and you're in yesterday's clothes; if you're a last-minute substitute for the best speaker in the country; if you have the flu with a 101-degree temperature, don't mention it. Don't apologize for your slides being upside down, for the room being too hot or too cold.

Don't apologize for *anything*. The minute you apologize, your ability to influence the audience goes down. Do everything you can to make sure none of those negatives happen, but if they do, *go on*.

Start your speech with power. Don't let the audience start off by thinking this is going to be a less-than-perfect experience. On the other hand, if an obvious disturbance is distracting everyone, don't ignore it. Suppose there's a ruckus next door. Say something like this to acknowledge it: "Sounds as if my speech is a big hit over there, too."

As you present your speech, keep in mind this familiar slogan: "Tell them what you're going to tell them, tell them, and then tell them what you just told them." Also let them know what you expect at the end of the presentation—the question-and-answer session, say, or the reception, or the cards you want them to fill out before they leave.

As you structure your message, think about the attention cycle of your audience and how you can address that with your pacing. It can be discouraging to look into the audience and see drooping eyelids, slumping bodies, or yawns. Worse yet is if people are walking out! If this happens, you've obviously lost the audience's attention. But there are ways you can recapture it.

Studies show that material at the beginning and end of a presentation will be remembered more than what's in the middle. It's interesting to note that people used to sit for long stretches and listen to speeches. Abraham Lincoln, Frederick Douglass, Ralph Waldo Emerson, and other nineteenth-century spellbinders often gave speeches lasting three or four hours. But in this era of MTV and sound bites, you're doing well if you can hold people for thirty minutes.

Whatever the length of your presentation, your audience's attention will go in cycles from *more* to *less* to *more* again during your speech. So how do you *hold* people's attention at the highest possible level? Simply by creating a lot of minicycles with beginnings, middles, and ends, instead of having one big cycle that lasts the entire presentation. You can do that with pacing.

Plan a change of pace every ten to fifteen minutes to liven up your talk and keep the audience's attention riveted. You do that through humor, stories, exercises that require people to move their bodies—even if it's just raising their hands—or requests for a verbal response.

You want to keep these change-of-pace techniques as physical as possible if your speech takes place after lunch or dinner. My mentor, Bill Gove, was a master at structuring his talks to be both flexible and interesting. For each key point in his speech, he had a string of stories or examples, all linked like a strand of pearls. He could seamlessly drop or add these "pearls" and thus tailor the talk to the audience and the time available. That way, he held the audience's attention and could give a cogent speech of any length.

Besides changing your pace frequently, here are four other ways to make it easier for listeners to remember more of your message:

Repetition means restating your main idea frequently. Of course, you should use different words to keep the presentation from being redundant or boring. Find as many ways as you can to state the Big Idea, including telling stories and creating images.

A classic example was Al Gore's vice-presidential acceptance speech to the 1992 Democratic National Convention. He lambasted then-President George Bush and Vice-President Dan Quayle on numerous issues, each time ending the criticism with "It's time for them to go!" As he neared the end of his talk, Gore was baiting the audience—"What time is it?"—and getting the thunderous, repeated response: "It's time for them to go!"

Association means making connections between what you're explaining and something that the listener already understands. Analogies to sports or cooking or some other universal topic will help the audience grasp and remember your message.

For instance, look at the number of sports coaches—such as Don Shula, Pat Riley, Rick Pitino, and Tommy Lasorda—who now speak and write about motivating yourself or others. They're using sports stories and sports metaphors, but their message is aimed at the business executive bent on motivating employees or at individuals seeking self-improvement.

Intensity, controlled by your tone of voice, conveys the passion you have about your message. Listen to the rolling, poetic, almost hypnotic cadences of Dr. Martin Luther King or Reverend Jesse Jackson, for example.

It's almost impossible not to be drawn in emotionally by the sonorous sound of their words.

Another way to intensify the content of your speech is by telling a gripping story. Even if you're speaking about a general topic, such as literacy or the need for more profits, the story of a single individual or an eye-opening statistic can dramatically underscore your point. Ronald Reagan was a genius at that.

The right visual aids, which we'll get to in a moment, also can add intensity to your talk.

Involvement means appealing to as many of your listeners' senses as possible. People have different ways of processing information. Some folks are predominantly visual. For others, hearing is stronger than seeing.

So you can use hand gestures, sound effects, and other multisensory devices during your speech to appeal to them. One well-known public speaker used to fly a small toy plane over the heads of the audience to make a point.

Another such tool for involvement is using exercises, such as small-group discussions or workbooks. One prominent speaker, Dr. John Lee, often speaks to groups about the importance in problem-solving of having the "big picture," of knowing your goal before starting work. But he really drives the point home by passing out puzzles for small groups in the audience to solve. One group—just one—also gets a picture of what the completed puzzle should look like. That last group *always* finishes first, making Lee's point more effectively than mere words possibly could.

Many speakers have a dynamite introduction and a powerful message, only to drop the ball at the end. So you also need a strong *conclusion*. This is when you'll sum up and stress the main ideas you want the audience to remember. You also encourage the appropriate action.

When you say, "In closing . . ." or "Let's review the main points we've covered. . . ." you give listeners a chance to reaffirm their understanding of your main points. Thus, your conclusion should be strong, succinct, and persuasive. Often, for the best result, it should be a funny or poignant story that underscores the speech's main theme. In fact, so important is the close that many speakers prefer to write it out word-for-word.

6. Practicing and Visualizing

You know your aim and your audience. You've prepared your material and honed the Big Idea until it's sure to get people's attention. Now you need to *practice* your delivery. It's important to rehearse out loud and to record yourself on either video or audio tape.

This is the fastest way to improve. You'll hear how you sound to others, detecting and eventually eliminating the *uh*s and *you know*s that pock the speeches of amateurs. You'll also be able to check your timing because you read out loud more slowly than you read in your mind. Reading out loud will also help you to see where the material is awkward—where it doesn't sound like you, where it "bumps" instead of flows.

Practice your speech at least four or five times. But don't memorize it. If you memorize, you may end up sounding stale because you are concentrating on the words instead of the presentation style.

If possible, rehearse in the actual location. That allows you to explore your physical mobility on the stage or in the board room or office. You also get a sense of the lighting and sound level, and you can practice with your audiovisual materials.

Of course, rehearsing on location isn't always possible. But don't let that stop you from rehearsing. Have family members and friends act as your audience. Ask them how you looked, and have them explain what they heard. Ask them what you can do better. If you have access to a video camera—many camera shops rent them by the day—tape yourself, then watch especially for eye contact and how your concepts come across.

The final part of your preparation involves *visualizing*, or imagining, yourself making a successful speech. Like a champion athlete, you can use visualization to reach your peak performance. Visualizing gives you a chance to experience success. And each time you experience success, you become more confident and expert in your delivery. The secret is to visualize with as much sensory detail as possible.

Begin by sitting in a comfortable position and closing your eyes. See the room. See yourself walking to the front of the room and being greeted by a warm round of applause. See the audience and feel them anxiously awaiting your message. Hear yourself begin, strongly and confidently. Watch the alert, interested faces as your audience readily surrenders its attention to you. Notice how they think about your words, laugh at your humor, nod in agreement with your main points.

Go through your entire presentation in your mind's eye. See the audience rise and give you a standing ovation when you finish. Relish your pleasure as people come up to tell you how well you did and how important the message was to them. Bask in your success.

Then repeat the visualization as often as you can until you truly experience being there and speaking well in your imagination.

NONVERBAL COMMUNICATORS

Beyond the standard visual aids that we're all familiar with, there's an important "visual aid" that we're less aware of: the nonverbal gestures you include in your presentation. Your body movements, facial expressions, and gestures reveal much more than words alone do about your emotional state. In other words, *how* you say something is as important as what you say.

The *eyes*, for example, are known as windows to the soul. It's been discovered that speakers who were rated "sincere" looked at their audiences an average of three times longer than speakers who were rated "insincere."

Get your *face* involved in the act! Delivering your material with an unchanged facial expression is as bad as delivering it in a monotone voice. Watch yourself in a mirror—it's hard to do, I know. But it's well worth it. Is your smile phony? Do you look overly serious? Is your face frozen like a mask, or animated in a way that'll capture your listeners' attention?

We also communicate through our *hands*. If your hands are tightly clenched into fists or clasped together rigidly, you're communicating that you're nervous. When you're proud of what you're saying, you usually show your hands quite openly. When you're not feeling good, you probably put your hands in your pockets or behind your back.

Watch your *arms* and *legs*. Crossed arms act as a protective guard against an anticipated attack. You convey readiness when you put your hands on your hips. You communicate thoughtfulness when you put one hand to your chin and rest your elbow in the other hand. And in terms of your legs, walking around on the stage communicates that you're comfortable with yourself and you're open with the audience.

Yet another nonverbal power communicator is good *posture*. Standing tall with your shoulders relaxed and open gives off a message of health and self-confidence.

So don't let being in front of people take away your natural body language. You have something important to say, and body language is one of the most effective tools for doing it. Find the gestures that feel natural and reinforce your presentation. Make bold rather than timid gestures and use broad as well as subtle movement.

VOCAL QUALITIES

Oddly, most people don't even consider their voice as part of their public image. But ask Pete Wilson about that. As governor of California, he sought the 1996 Republican presidential nomination at a time when minor throat surgery left him with little more than a croak for three months. His campaign nosedived.

"People were so distracted by the voice quality that they weren't able to pay any attention," he recalled. "I saw looks of absolute horror on their faces. . . . People would ask, 'Does it hurt?' And I'd say, 'Only to listen.'"

One voice expert, Dr. Carol Fleming, points out that what you sound like indicates your personality, suggests your intelligence level, and reveals a lot about your background. Consider, she says, how much we learn in the first few seconds talking on the phone with a stranger: their gender, their approximate age, and their general temperament. You might also make a good guess about the person's regional or ethnic background or even a judgment about their credibility and confidence. That's a lot to know about a person in less than five seconds!

So, obviously, when you give a speech, there's a lot more that's communicated to your audience. Consider these major vocal qualities:

Resonance. Does the sound come from deep in your throat, or is your voice thin and weak as happens when the sounds come only from your mouth, not your whole upper body? Having resonance allows you to fill a space with your voice without having to raise your volume level.

Rhythm. This is the flow of your words. Do they connect smoothly with each other or sound choppy and separate? If your sentences are choppy—if you hesitate and then start a new idea in the middle of another one—it sounds as if you're not thinking very clearly.

Speed. How fast do you talk? Most people who have problems with the speed of their presentations talk too fast. We all know the stereotype of "the fast talker" as someone not to be trusted. On the other hand, speaking too slowly can be tedious, and it's often interpreted to mean that the speaker thinks rather slowly. The point is: Be aware of the speed at which you talk and, to sustain interest, vary that pace.

Pitch. This means how high or low your voice is. This is difficult to change without some professional help from a speech consultant or a singing coach. But fortunately, most of us have a voice that falls into a normal pitch range.

Volume. Do you speak too loudly, or too softly? That may be hard to tell from a tape recording because you can adjust the volume on the machine. Ask someone you trust to give you good feedback. Again, as you speak, vary your volume to keep your audience alert.

Inflection. Check for vocal variety, or the pitch changes in your voice as you speak. Are some words emphasized with more volume? Do you hold other words longer to give them more importance? Or does everything sound about the same? A monotone, or flatness in a voice, makes your talk boring.

Clarity. Are each of your words distinct? Or do they run together? This is something men need to pay special attention to because males tend to mumble more than women. The secret here is using your lips. Mumblers tend not to move their lips, and thus, one has to listen closely in order to get what they're saying.

Pauses. Skillful speakers use silence to tease, titillate, intrigue, manipulate, and control. Pauses allow the audience to absorb your wisdom and underscore your best points. Renowned speaking coach Ron Arden says pauses encourage audiences to picture the images you evoke and promote an "inner dialogue" in their mind (e.g., "That's fascinating!" or "What a great idea; I must remember that!" or even "I don't agree with that.")

Arden has identified nine types of pauses, but for our purposes, the most important are:

Sense pause: One-half to one full second in length, these pauses—similar to a comma in writing—break your words into parcels that make sense, helping the listener absorb and relate to what he's hearing.

Transitional pause: One to two seconds long, this separates one thought from another, much as a period does in writing. Without this pause, thoughts tend to run into one another, leaving the listener confused and off balance.

Reflective pause: This two-to-four-second pause is used after you've said something unusual, complex, important, or provocative. In effect, it signals, "I've put this long silence here because I believe it's important that you think about what I just said." But you must "earn" this pause. If what it follows is not worth reflecting on, the listener soon will get bored and feel let down.

Dramatic pause: Three seconds or longer, this creates anticipation for, say, a punch line or a startling statistic. In effect, the speaker teases the audience by saying, "I'm going to dangle something for you here—wait for it!" Again, it must be earned by following it with something of substance. Audiences love to be teased, but only if the result is worth it.

Dr. Carol Fleming, whom I mentioned before, advises that if you want to improve your vocal image, start with just one aspect. Changing vocal patterns that have been in place for years takes time and conscious attention. As you listen to your recording of yourself, decide which aspect needs the most improvement.

TONE OF VOICE

Perhaps you remember your rebellious teenage years when your mom would say, "Don't speak to me in that tone of voice!" Tone is another aspect of your voice that's slippery to describe but easy to hear. In fact, your tone often has more impact than your actual words.

"In the right key, one can say anything. In the wrong key nothing," said playwright George Bernard Shaw. "The only delicate part is the establishment of the key."

Our pets are a great example of this. They'll respond

positively to anything said in a sweet, loving voice. But if you say harshly, "You're a wonderful dog, Spot, and I'm going to give you a special treat," Spot will react poorly. Similarly, people react to vocal tone as much as or more than they do to words.

Your tone of voice communicates a lot about you and your personality. Many people have no idea that their voice conveys harshness, or irritability, or a patronizing attitude, until they hear it played back on tape.

A positive tone of voice can be a very effective part of winning someone else's trust and cooperation. If your tone is pleasant, confident, and cheerful, you encourage those qualities in the listener. You can also convey qualities such as competence, leadership, and strength with your tone.

JUMP-STARTING YOUR PUBLIC-SPEAKING SKILLS

So there's a lot to think about when it comes to being a polished presenter. Maybe you have some of the skills I covered, and need to concentrate on a few others. Just know that with practice, most of this will become second nature to you, like riding a bicycle. But mastery won't come overnight. Remember, there was a fair amount of trial and error before you sped down the street on your two-wheeler.

Here are some other tricks of the trade:

1. *Care—really care—about your subject.* Passion is the starting point of all good public speaking. Peggy Noonan, President Reagan's celebrated speechwriter, describes a speech as "poetry: cadence, rhythm, imagery,

sweep! [It] reminds us that words, like children, have the power to make dance the dullest beanbag of a heart."

So pick a subject that has an inordinate impact on you, a subject you'd like to share with others because you know, intensely, that they could benefit from your knowledge. Your enthusiasm will show through, and all the following pointers will come more easily.

Do not be one of those speakers of whom Churchill once said, "Before they get up, they do not know what they are going to say; when they are speaking, they do not know what they are saying; and when they have sat down, they do not know what they have said."

2. *Be brief.* The best way to impress an audience is to finish early. "My father gave me this advice on speech making," said James Roosevelt, son of FDR: "Be sincere . . . be brief . . . be seated." Remember, in the electronic age, many people have the attention span of a flashcube. So be sure you know your Big Idea, hit it hard, hit it well, finish strong, and, for maximum impression, keep it short. The less opportunity you give your audience's minds to wander, the more they'll appreciate you and remember what you had to say.

3. *Find out where the land mines are—and avoid them.* Find out who's spoken to the same group and ask them what worked and what they'd do differently. Do you need razzmatazz audiovisuals? Or is it a more cerebral group that'll just want the facts? Can the host be counted on to give a decent introduction? (If not, you might want to write one for him or her.)

4. *Make use of memory joggers.* You can keep attention high and help people remember your message if you use ample *examples* to transmit your mes-

sage powerfully. Similarly, *statistics*, if used sparingly and presented simply, can add drama and credibility to your message. *Comparisons* can help your audience evaluate different options quickly and logically, and *testimony*—personal stories of credible people—can make your message more memorable and believable.

5. ***Bad visual aids are worse than none at all.*** Your audience is sure to be impressed by your visual aids—but will it be a *good* impression? Visual aids, if well done, can help you appear confident, professional, and persuasive. But poorly done, they can contradict everything you've tried to accomplish with your words.

The most common mistake is putting too much information on one image. Each visual aid should focus on one idea. Another common error is using the visual aid as a cue card and reading the information. Because the audience can read faster than you can talk, this is *boring*!

A third mistake is using the wrong type of visual aid. Flip charts and white boards are best with small, informal groups; overhead transparencies work well with medium-sized groups; and slides usually get the best response from large, formal audiences.

6. ***Drum the purpose of your talk into your brain.*** Summarize the "why?"—the Big Idea—of your talk in one sentence, write it on a three-by-five card, and keep it in front of you as you prepare your speech. That'll keep you on track as you write and practice.

7. ***Rattle-proof yourself.*** Eamon de Valera, an Irish political firebrand, was once arrested and jailed while giving a speech. Released after a year, he summoned a

meeting in the same spot and began, "As I was saying when I was interrupted . . ."

That's an interruption you hopefully won't have to endure. But, sooner or later, you'll probably experience other unexpected events, such as a power failure, an earthquake, a breakdown of audiovisual gear, or a major disturbance—say, someone having a heart attack—in the audience. The key to retaining your poise is to know your presentation so well that you won't lose your concentration, even if everyone else does temporarily.

Once I was giving a speech to a large audience in a Florida hotel ballroom and the power went out—completely! There we all were, several hundred people and me, in total darkness. I just kept speaking as if nothing was amiss. After several minutes—and just as I was telling a tale about a character looking for "a sign from above," or something to that effect, the lights came on. The audience cheered wildly, as if I'd arranged the whole thing. And I, of course, breathed a huge sigh of relief. Score one for chutzpah!

8. *Remember the pause that refreshes.* The sweet sound of silence, the power of the pause, can be artfully used in any speech. Pauses are not really empty spaces. Instead, they're opportunities for the audience to respond to your words with their own thoughts, images, and feelings.

Listeners react negatively when they feel as if they're being verbally machine-gunned. But pauses give them time to consider and digest what's being said—and give you the chance to call attention to your most interesting points.

If you naturally tend toward a rapid pace, insert written reminders into your speech to *Pause* or *Slow Down.* "The right word may be effective," Mark Twain said, "but no word was ever as effective as a rightly timed pause."

9. *Make light.* In all but the most grave of talks (such as the threat of nuclear war or the spread of AIDS), humor is vital. It can underline points, reduce tension, relieve pressure, and enhance persuasion. It takes humor to make a presentation complete.

But there's a wrong way and a right way to do it. Many speakers begin with a joke—and that may be reason alone not to do so. It may be better to save your humor until you've gotten the audience tuned in to who you are, what you sound like, and what you've got to say.

Some pointers about using humor:

- Keep your stories fresh and adjust details to fit the occasion and the audience. Susan RoAne, a keynote speaker and author of *How to Work a Room*, recommends the "AT&T" rule for choosing humor: Is it Appropriate? Is it Tasteful? And is it Timely?
- Select material that lends itself to telling. Leave out the "he said" or "she said." Instead, impersonate the characters talking to each other.
- Don't go overboard laughing at your own material, but *do* signal the audience that entertaining material is on the way by enjoying the telling, having a sparkle in your eye and an air of suppressed glee about you as you speak.
- Rehearse . . . and rehearse . . . and rehearse!

10. *Don't dawdle at the finish line.* Good speakers understand that the end is just as important—and maybe more so—as the beginning. This is your chance to sum up your best thoughts, words, and images and

imprint them indelibly on the audience's collective brain.

Don't miss that opportunity by running beyond your time limit, or fumbling your final message. Know what you want to say, say it, and then say good night.

Chapter 5

◆

LISTENING ATTENTIVELY

Have you ever been to a dinner party where you sensed the talk wasn't really a conversation as much as a series of monologues? First, somebody tells about their vacation, and maybe a dutiful but shallow question or two is asked. Then somebody else brags about his kid getting into medical school, which leads another guest to talk about her own college days. On and on it goes, while eyes wander and heads occasionally nod between bites of quiche and sips of French Colombard.

You get the impression no one is really listening. Rather, they're just rehearsing what they might say. Maybe they're thinking about how to sound good, how strongly to make their points, or how to outshine the others. As a result, by evening's end, everyone will have talked—but people really won't have communicated much or gotten to know each other very well.

Unfortunately, many of our everyday conversations are like that, too. While we *hear*, we only pretend to listen. Listening doesn't just mean shutting up while someone else speaks—though that's a start. ("A good listener is a good talker with a sore throat," one English wit said.)

But listening—*real* listening—takes more work than that. It's more than the physical process of hearing. It also takes intellectual and emotional effort. To get a full appreciation of the other person and what's being said, you need to ask questions, give feedback, remain objective, figure out what's really being said and what's not being said, and observe and interpret body language.

As Matthew McKay and Martha Davis say in their book, *How to Communicate*, "Listening is a commitment and a compliment. It's a commitment to understanding how other people feel, how they see their world" and it's "a compliment because it says to the other person: 'I care about what's happening to you, your life and your experience are important.'"

HOW GOOD A LISTENER ARE YOU?

When we think of people who have charisma, we probably think of people who talk well. And indeed, in the previous chapter we emphasized the importance of vocal image, vocal quality, and effective public speaking.

But that's only half the picture. When you want to win someone's attention and gain his or her confidence, listening is just as important as speaking. Good listening draws people to you; poor listening causes them to drift away. Find someone with charisma, and without a doubt, you've found an accomplished listener.

Poor listening is an acknowledged problem between

employees and bosses, salespeople and customers, children and parents, husbands and wives. Lack of effective listening also leads to lost clients, lost political campaigns, and lost causes.

In fact, leadership is practically impossible for the person who can't listen effectively. Miscommunication, mistakes, and work that needs to be redone are common by-products of poor listening. One University of Minnesota study showed that nearly 60 percent of misunderstandings in the business world can be traced to poor listening and only 1 percent to written communication.

In addition, there's another big drawback to poor listening: People view poor listeners as self-centered, disinterested, preoccupied, and aloof. "Man's inability to communicate is a result of his failure to listen effectively, skillfully, and with understanding to another person," said famed psychologist Carl Rogers.

On the other hand, learning to listen better can transform people and relationships by:

- Making others feel appreciated and valued because you make the effort to share their excitement and ideas.
- Saving time by reducing mistakes and misunderstandings.
- Increasing trust, credibility, and cooperation.
- Helping solve problems more quickly.

It's been said that we listen more than we do any other human activity, except breathe. And most of us probably think we're better listeners than we are.

But few of us listen as effectively as we should. And since the average worker spends three-quarters of each day verbally communicating and more than half of that listening, there's a lot at stake. In this chapter, you'll learn how to hone your skills as a listener, and, thus, increase your charisma.

QUICK QUIZ: YOUR LISTENING SKILLS

For each pair of statements below, distribute three points between the two alternatives (A and B), depending on how characteristic of you the statement is. Although some pairs of statements may seem equally true for you, assign more points to the alternative that is more representative of your behavior most of the time.

Examples:

- If A is very characteristic of you and B is very uncharacteristic, write "3" next to A and "0" next to B.
- If A is more characteristic of you than B, write "2" next to A and "1" next to B.
- If B is very characteristic of you and A is very uncharacteristic, write "3" next to B and "0" next to A.

. . . and so on.

1A___I almost always remember what people have recently said to me, and thus am able to impress them by later calling up such small details in conversation with them.

1B___I frequently forget details of what people have said and find myself asking them to repeat.

2A___I'm pretty good at concentrating on speakers' words and meaning.

2B___I tend to argue with speakers mentally, or plan my reply, or jump ahead and try to figure out where they're going with their remarks before they actually get there.

3A___I can usually listen dispassionately to what people are saying.

3B___I often feel myself emotionally reacting to what people are saying before they've finished.

4A___Though tempted, I almost never interrupt someone who's talking.

4B___I do sometimes interrupt because I believe a fruitful dialogue requires that I make some points as they occur to me and at the point where they'll do the most good.

5A__I often take notes, physically or mentally, on what someone says so that I can respond fully when he or she is done.

5B__I easily get the gist of what someone is saying without taking notes, which might interfere with my concentration.

6A___I make a determined effort not to judge people until I've heard all of what they have to say.

6B___I'm a good judge of character and I can often get a good "read" on people before the conversation is over.

7A___I acknowledge people's remarks with nods of the head, smiles or frowns, exclamations, or whatever other response shows them that I'm alert and understanding them.

7B___I concentrate on what the other person is saying rather than trying to send all sorts of signals before they're done.

8A___When someone is having a conversation with me, I usually turn off the radio or TV, hold my calls, wait to return E-mail, and otherwise minimize disruptions.

8B___I'm capable of doing several things at once while still listening attentively to others.

9A___In conversations, I maintain steady eye contact with the person speaking.

9B___I frequently avert my glance so as not to be intimidating to the speaker.

10A___I avoid fidgeting, cracking knuckles, stretching, jingling keys, or other mannerisms while someone is talking.

10B___I make the talker as comfortable as possible by trying to act naturally, which means adhering to my normal mannerisms.

SCORING:

Please add point totals under "A" and enter here: _____

Please add point totals under "B" and enter here: _____

Now let's take a look at how you scored on this segment. If your "A" score is significantly greater than your "B" score (and if you were truly honest!), you are fairly strong in this aspect of charisma. The more lopsided your "A" score, the better listener you are. If your "A" score exceeds your "B" by, say, a 2-to-1 margin, your listening "glass" is far fuller than most.

Conversely, if your "B" score approximates your "A" score, you may have identified an improvement opportunity. And if the "B" score is higher than your "A," that's an indication that you need lots of work in this area.

ROADBLOCKS TO EFFECTIVE LISTENING

There are five basic reasons we fail to listen well.

First, listening takes effort. As I said, it's more than just keeping quiet. It means really concentrating on the other person. An active listener registers increased blood pressure, a higher pulse rate, and more perspiration. Because it takes so much effort, a lot of people just don't listen.

Second, there's now enormous competition for our attention from radio, TV, movies, computers, books and magazines, and much more. With all these incoming stimuli, we've learned to screen out information we deem irrelevant. Unfortunately, we also screen out things that are important.

Here's a *third* reason why we don't listen well: We think we already know what someone is going to say. We assume that we have a full understanding right from the start, so we jump in and interrupt. We don't take the time required to hear people out.

The *fourth* reason has to do with the speed gap— the difference between how fast we talk and how fast we listen. The average person speaks at about 135 to 175 words a minute, but comprehends at 400 to 500 words a minute. For the person who's not listening well, that's plenty of time to jump to conclusions, day-dream, plan a reply, or mentally argue with the speaker. At least that's how poor listeners spend the time.

And the *fifth* reason we don't listen well is because *we don't know how*. We do more listening than speaking, reading, or writing. But I bet you've never had a course in listening, have you?

I think listening is the most neglected and least understood of all the aspects of communication. And, largely, this weak link springs from bad habits. In short, we haven't been trained to listen.

An untrained listener is likely to understand and retain only 50 percent of a conversation moments after it's finished. This retention rate drops to an even less impressive 25 percent just 48 hours later. So an untrained listener's recall of a conversation that took place more than a couple of days ago will always be incomplete and usually inaccurate. No wonder people seldom agree about what's been discussed!

LEVELS OF LISTENING

We typically listen at one of four basic levels of attentiveness. Do you recognize yourself or any of your
associates?

1. *The Nonlistener* is someone who doesn't actually
hear the speaker at all. In fact, no real effort is made to
hear what the other person is saying. Indeed, it's pretty
obvious that this person is not really paying any
attention. Blank stares and nervous mannerisms usually
greet your attempt to make a point. Sometimes this
person fakes attention while thinking about unrelated
matters. But before long, it's clear that his or her
attention is elsewhere.

Nonlisteners really want to do all, or most of, the
speaking. They constantly interrupt and think they
always must have the last word. They're usually considered social bores and know-it-alls, and they're typically disliked or merely tolerated.

2. *The Marginal Listener* is a superficial listener. He
or she hears the sounds and words—but not the
meaning and intent. Marginal listeners stay on the
surface of the conversation or issue, never risking to go
deeper.

They can't listen closely to what's being said now
because they're too busy thinking about what they
want to say next. Marginal listeners are easily distracted. In fact, many marginal listeners *look* for outside
distractions—an incoming phone call, say, or an E-mail
message on the computer screen—to use as an excuse
for pulling themselves away from the conversation.

They prefer to evade difficult presentations or discussions, and when they do listen, they tend to listen

only for the bottom line instead of the overall message. In fact, when you've finished your statement, the marginal listener, having missed the nuances, the body language, and much of the content itself, is likely to say, "So what's the point?"

Marginal listening is especially dangerous because of the enormous possibility for misunderstanding. At least at Level 1—nonlistening—the speaker receives many clues that the other person isn't tuning in to the conversation. But at the marginal listening level, the speaker may be lulled into a false sense of security that he or she is in fact being listened to and understood.

Marginal listening is a staple of television sitcoms and film comedies. One character, only half listening, does something very different from what's intended, creating an absurd situation. Invariably, the hapless character ends up saying something like, "But I *thought* you said . . ."

But in real life, it isn't funny. Marginal listeners are insulting to the speaker because they merely feign interest. And bad things—accidents, waste, embarrassments—can occur because the poor listener doesn't really hear the speaker's message.

3. *The Technical Listener* actively tries to hear what the speaker is saying. So this is the label most of us would give ourselves if we consider ourselves to be "good" listeners. More concentration and attention are required at this level.

However, technical listeners still don't make an effort to understand the speaker's *intent*. They tend to be logical listeners, more concerned about content than feelings. They judge the message merely on what's said, totally ignoring the part of the message that's carried in the speaker's vocal intonation, body language, and facial expressions. They're great with semantics, facts, and statistics, but poor in terms of sensitivity, empathy, and true understanding.

In other words, technical listeners believe that they understand the speaker—but the speaker doesn't feel understood.

> I know you think you understand what I
> said. But I don't think you understand that
> what I said is not what I meant.

That may sound like a line from an Abbott and Costello skit. But actually, you've probably had lots of conversations like this in which you were trying to extricate yourself from a communications snafu, or someone else was.

This is a common by-product of the tremendous speed gap I mentioned earlier. The mind is capable of listening and thinking at a rate up to three times the speed of talking. The technical listener is using that time gap to frame his or her response or to count the number of times the speaker says "you know."

Again, this is the level of listening that people employ in most everyday conversations. It's a truly difficult habit to break.

4. *The Active Listener* is unquestionably at the most powerful level of listening. Active listening is also the most demanding and tiring because it requires the most mental and emotional effort.

The active listener refrains from judging the speaker's message, and instead focuses on understanding his or her *point of view*. So the active listener concentrates on the thoughts and feelings of the speaker—including what's *not* being said—as well as the actual words.

To listen actively means suspending your personal thoughts and feelings. It means giving attention solely to the speaker. It means sending out verbal and non-verbal feedback that tells the speaker you're absorbing what's being said.

This is important. If you expect to get the speaker's support, he or she needs to know they're being heard.

THE SIX SKILLS OF ACTIVE LISTENING

To reach this highest level of listening proficiency, you need to develop six separate skills. I've combined them into the easy-to-remember acronym CARESS:

Concentrate. Focus your attention on the speaker, and *only* on the speaker.

Acknowledge. When you acknowledge the other person, you show your interest and attention.

Research and respond. Gather information about the other person, including his or her interests and objectives.

Exercise emotional control. Deal with highly charged messages in a thoughtful manner and wait until the entire message is received before reacting.

Sense the nonverbal message. Be aware of what the speaker is saying with his or her body language and gestures.

Structure. Organize the information as you receive

it. This is what you do with the time gap between speaking and hearing speeds.

Let's look at each of these skills in more detail.

Concentrate Completely
on the Speaker

You must eliminate noise and distractions. These barriers may be in the environment, like noises in the room, other people talking, poor acoustics, bad odors, extreme temperatures, an uncomfortable chair, or visual distractions. Or they could be physical disruptions such as telephone calls or visitors.

Another kind of barrier is something distracting about the speaker. Maybe he or she dresses oddly, shows poor grooming, has disturbing mannerisms, confusing facial expressions or body language. Or perhaps he or she has a thick accent or an unappealing presentation style.

Yet another barrier has to do with you, the listener, and can be either physical or psychological. Maybe it's close to lunch or quitting time, and you're preoccupied with how you feel. You're hungry or tired, or angry, or maybe have a cold or a toothache. If so, you're not going to be listening fully.

Another physical barrier could be your proximity to the speaker. If he or she's either too close or too far away from you, you may feel uncomfortable and have a hard time concentrating.

A second sort of internal barrier is psychological. Perhaps you're closed-minded to new ideas or resistant to information that runs contrary to your beliefs and values. Or maybe you're bored, or daydreaming, or jumping to conclusions.

Ways to Minimize Distractions

So there are lots of potential distractions, internal and external. If you can't avoid them, minimize them. You do that by focusing totally on the speaker and paying attention. Here are four specific techniques that will help you concentrate while listening:

1. *Take a deep breath*. This will prevent you from interrupting, and will provide your brain with invigorating oxygen. Try it now, and as you're doing it, try to speak. It doesn't work very well, does it?

2. *Consciously decide to listen*. No matter who's speaking, pay attention and listen for information that's particularly interesting or useful. You never know what you might learn. As show-biz wit Wilson Mizner once said, "A good listener is not only popular everywhere, but after a while he knows something."

3. *Mentally paraphrase what the speaker is saying*. This will prevent you from daydreaming about irrelevant and superfluous topics. You'll concentrate on the speaker instead of yourself.

4. *Maintain eye contact*. Where your eyes focus, your ears follow. You're most likely to listen to what you are looking at.

So, if you can't eliminate a distraction, use one or more of these techniques—breathe deeply, decide to listen, paraphrase, or maintain eye contact. They'll help you handle the distractions.

Acknowledging the Speaker

This is the second technique of the CARESS model. Think about how you like to be listened to. What are the important responses you look for in other people when *they* are listening to *you*? Here are four things most people mention:

First, eye contact. As we just discussed, this is a sign of attention. When you don't have eye contact with your listener, you may feel like you're talking to a brick wall.

Second, verbal responses and vocal participation such as, "Hmm," "Yeah," "Wow!" and "No kidding?" These show interest in what's being said.

Third, other acknowledging gestures such as smiling, nodding one's head, leaning forward with interest, directly facing the speaker, and appropriate facial expressions or body language. All of these gestures say, in effect, "I'm really interested in what you have to say." Speakers like to see that.

And, the *fourth* kind of acknowledgment is making clarifying remarks that restate the speaker's points, such as "If I understand you correctly, you're saying that . . ." or "In other words, the biggest hurdles are . . ."

Use these techniques, and you'll show courtesy to the speaker. Equally important, you'll enrich yourself by joining in a give-and-take that increases your understanding.

Researching

"Researching" is what makes a conversation a two-way street. And it's this two-way flow that creates a meeting of the minds between the speaker and the listener.

Researching, as the term is used here, involves

asking questions and giving feedback, and it serves many purposes. For example, it allows you to clarify a message, enlarge upon a subject, or go into a particular topic in more depth. It allows you to get the speaker to change the direction of the conversation. Or it can prompt the speaker to vent feelings of anger, excitement, enthusiasm, and so on. And it also allows you to support and reinforce particular parts of a speaker's message.

A listener who doesn't ask questions, give feedback, or make comments at the appropriate time isn't really participating. This creates an information imbalance that can, at best, make the speaker uncomfortable and, at worst, make for major misunderstandings.

A story is told, for example, about former FBI director J. Edgar Hoover, who had strong feelings on many subjects, including how internal reports were formatted. Annoyed that a certain report writer hadn't followed the guidelines, he scribbled at the top of the first page *Watch the borders*. The report with the boss's notation made the rounds. No one quite understood, but no one asked the intimidating Mr. Hoover, either.

So word went out to FBI field offices to "watch the borders"—and extra agents were deployed all along the Mexican and Canadian frontiers. Only later was the truth learned: Hoover was objecting to the size of the margins the writer had used on his memo.

This same sort of misunderstanding is common in oral communications, too, when nobody checks to clarify the information. All it takes is a simple question to make sure we understand clearly. For instance, studies of the *Challenger* space tragedy show there may have been as many as 1,100 people who knew about the potential danger of failure of the O-ring. But either no one brought it up or no one was listening when they did.

Asking the right questions at the right time and responding appropriately to the speaker is an essential part of active listening. Skillful questioning simplifies the listener's job because it gets the speaker to "open up," to reveal hidden feelings, motives, needs, goals, and desires.

Exercise Emotional Control

What causes an emotional overreaction? It's generally prompted by the speaker himself or by something he or she says. For instance, going to an elegant party dressed like a bum might influence the hosts negatively. On the other hand, wearing a high-powered, Wall Street–like suit might put a rural businessperson on the defensive against a supposedly not-to-be-trusted city slicker.

Severe emotional overreaction can also be caused by loaded topics, such as ethnic, racial, religious, or political references. Differences in values, beliefs, attitudes, education, speed of delivery, image, and a host of other factors can cause a disruption in communication.

So, as listeners, we tend to tune out when we see or hear something we don't like. As a result, we often miss the true substance of what's being said.

When your emotional reaction begins, you'll have an almost irresistible tendency to interrupt, to butt in, to argue. You may feel your pulse speed up, your breathing become more rapid, or your face become flushed. You may lose your train of thought. Once you recognize this negative emotional reaction, you can redirect it with the following techniques:

First, pause to delay your response or reaction. It's the tried-and-true approach of counting to ten, or taking in some long, deep breaths. These can really work to calm you down.

A *second* calming technique: Think about what you have in common with the speaker, rather than focusing on your differences. Maybe you don't disagree with the person's motivations—such as raising more money for the school. You just don't agree with her solutions.

And *third*, imagine yourself calm and relaxed. Think of a time in your past when you were laid-back, on top of the world, and feeling incredibly great. Visualize that experience as vividly as you can. When you exercise emotional control, you'll find that active listening is no longer a struggle.

Sense the Nonverbal Message

It's critical that you read the nonverbal messages in the speaker's communications. If you don't, you're missing a major aspect of his or her message. Remember our discussion about the nonverbal aspects of presentations.

Structure

Structuring the information is probably the most sophisticated of the listening techniques. As I said earlier, you can use the time gap created by differences in listening and speaking speeds to structure the message you're listening to. There are three ways to structure: indexing, sequencing, and comparing.

Indexing is like outlining—mentally or on paper— what the speaker says. It'll dramatically increase your comprehension and recall. You note the major idea, the key points, the subpoints, and so on. Indexing is made easier by listening for transitional phrases. When people say things like "for example," or "Let me elaborate on that," you know that a rationale, a subpoint, or a supporting point is likely to follow.

Sequencing is listening for order, or priority. Sometimes, such as when you're being given instructions, the sequence is crucial. So listen for words like *first, second, next,* or *then, last.* Don't be shy about double-checking with the speaker to make sure you understand the proper sequence or the relative weight that you should give each element.

Comparing, on the other hand, involves discriminating between what's fact and what's assumption, between advantages and disadvantages, and between positives and negatives. You also want to listen for consistency. Is what the speaker saying now consistent with what he or she said previously? This makes you a detective of sorts—it allows you to realize when something doesn't make sense. When it doesn't, then you need to ask questions to clear up any confusion.

For most of us, active listening means changing a lifetime's worth of poor listening habits. It means entering the other person's situation and trying to understand their frame of reference. Using the CARESS model can help you do just that.

Improving your listening habits is vital. That's because when I talk, I only know what I know. But when I listen, I not only know what I know, I also know what you know. Thus, *listening is power.*

JUMP-STARTING YOUR LISTENING SKILLS

Most of us have lots of room for improvement in our listening techniques. I encourage you to practice the methods I've just described in your very next conversation. Like anything new, they won't feel natural until you've used them a lot. But do so, and you'll definitely be on your way to improving this aspect of your charisma.

Meanwhile, here are some further ideas on ways to make active listening easier for you:

1. *Listen—really listen—to one person for one day.* Choose one person you could relate to better. Commit to listening to them—not just hearing them—for one day. After each meeting, ask yourself: Did I use the CARESS techniques? Did I really make an effort to go beyond superficialities? Did I observe verbal, vocal, and visual clues? Did I note what was not being said as well as what was said?

Once you've gotten into this habit of nudging yourself to listen better, extend this exercise to successive days, then to other acquaintances as well. Listening well is a gift you can give to others. It'll cost you nothing, but it may be invaluable to them.

2. *Create a receptive listening environment.* Turn off the TV. Hold your calls. Put away your spread sheets and silence your computer. When listening, forget about clipping your nails, crocheting, solving crossword puzzles, or snapping your chewing gum. Instead, try to provide a private, quiet, comfortable setting where you sit side by side with others

without distractions. If that's not possible, perhaps suggest a later meeting in a more neutral, quieter environment.

The point is to make your partner feel like you're there for him or her. Don't be like the boss who put a desk-sized model of a parking meter on his desk, then required employees to feed the meter—10 cents for every 10 minutes of conversation. What a signal he was sending out!

3. ***Don't talk when I'm interrupting.*** If someone else is interrupting, avoid the temptation to reply in kind. It'll just raise the level of acrimony and widen the gulf between you. Instead, be the one who shows restraint by listening to them, then quietly, calmly, taking up where you left off.

"If you're talking, you aren't learning," President Lyndon Johnson used to say. And by showing more courtesy than your adversary, you will be quietly sending a message as to how you both ought to be acting.

4. ***Don't overdo it.*** Sometimes newcomers to the skill of listening can get carried away. They know they're supposed to have eye contact, so they'll stare so much the speaker will feel intimidated. Taught to nod their heads to show they're comprehending, they'll start bobbing like sailboats on a rough sea. Having learned to project appropriate facial expressions while listening, they'll look as if they're suffering gastric distress.

Eventually, the speaker figures out that the other person recently attended a "listening" seminar or read a book on the subject. But it all comes across as artificial. All good things, including listening, require moderation and suitable application. Too much exaggerated listening is just as bad as, if not worse than, none at all.

5. *Practice mind-mapping.* An excellent method for note taking is "mind-mapping." This free-form technique helps you take notes quickly without breaking the flow of the conversation. Essentially, you use a rough diagram to connect primary pieces of information, then break it into appropriate subtopics or details.

It's extremely helpful and easy to use, and not at all like the old-fashioned Roman-numeral kind of outlining you probably learned in school. If you want to know more, I recommend an excellent book: Tony Buzan's *The Mind Map Book.*

6. *Be alert to your body language.* What you do with your eyes, face, hands, arms, legs, and posture sends out signals as to whether you are, or aren't, listening to and understanding what the other person is saying. For example, if you noticed someone you were talking to doing the following, what would you think?

- Glancing sideways
- Sighing
- Yawning
- Frowning
- Crossing arms on chest
- Looking at the ceiling
- Cleaning fingernails
- Cracking knuckles
- Jingling change or rattling keys
- Fidgeting in chair

You'd very quickly get the impression—wouldn't you?—that no matter what words come from this person's mouth, he or she actually has zero interest in what you're talking about and wishes you'd just go away. As Ralph Waldo Emerson said, "What you *are* is shouting so loud, I can't hear what you are saying."

Conversely, consider these mannerisms:

- Looking into your eyes
- Smiling frequently
- Raising eyebrows periodically
- Grinning at appropriate moments
- Using expressive hand gestures when speaking
- Keeping eyes wide open
- Licking lips
- Tilting head
- Leaning toward you

This person shows interest in you and what you're saying. In addition, the active listener usually acknowledges the speaker verbally as well with such comments as "I see," "Uh-huh," "Mmmm," or "Really?"

In a later chapter, you'll learn how some people are contact-oriented, while others are much less so, preferring more space between them and the person they're talking to. You'll be a better listener if you honor those spatial preferences.

Again, when you acknowledge the other person both verbally and nonverbally, you build trust and increase rapport. And you'll probably learn something, too!

7. *Abstain from judging.* As someone once advised, "Grow antennae, not horns." If you prejudge someone

as shallow or crazy or ill-informed, you automatically cease paying attention to what they say. So a basic rule of listening is to judge only after you've heard and evaluated what they say. Don't jump to conclusions based on how they look, or what you've heard about them, or whether they're nervous.

In fact, maybe a good exercise would be to go out of your way to listen to a difficult speaker. Maybe he talks with a thick accent. Or talks much more rapidly, or more slowly, than you, or uses a lot of big words. Whatever difficulty this speaker poses, seize it as an opportunity not to prejudge but to practice your listening skills. Given some time, you'll become more comfortable and effective in listening to diverse styles.

8. *Listen with empathy.* No matter how outrageous, inconsiderate, false, self-centered, or pompous the person you're talking to is, remember: He or she is simply trying to survive, just like you. We're all participating in the same physical and psychological struggle. Some of us just have better survival strategies than others. Thus, the obnoxious person deserves more pity than scorn. "The wounded deer leaps highest," Emily Dickinson wrote, and it's true.

So listening with empathy means asking yourself, "Where is this person's anger coming from?" "What is he or she asking for?" "What can I do that's reasonable and noncondemning?" You're not everyone's shrink, and you don't have to carry the weight of the world on your back.

But, on the other hand, if you can think through what makes this person behave like this, perhaps you'll be inclined to cut them a little slack. Genuinely listening well is, at its heart, an act of love, and as such, may help heal.

9. ***Be sensitive to emotional deaf spots.*** Deaf spots are words that make your mind wander or go off on a mental tangent. They automatically produce a mental barrier that impedes listening. Everybody is affected that way by certain words.

For example, a speaker giving a talk to savings-and-loan personnel kept saying "bank." To members of that industry, banks and S&Ls are very different things and so each reference to them as "bankers" irritated the audience and aroused emotions that temporarily derailed their listening.

So be alert to what your own deaf spots are and make adjustments. And try to find out what raises the hackles of other people, then avoid those words so as to raise the likely level of listening.

10. ***Create and use an active-listening attitude.*** Learning to be an active listener is like learning to be an active jogger. It takes effort. You start little by little and work upward. It's as much a state of mind as a physical activity. Besides, as you work longer and get better, it pays ever-increasing benefits.

An active-listening *attitude* can help tremendously in breaking your poor listening habits. Exercising such an attitude means:

- ***Appreciating that listening is as powerful as speech.*** What someone says to you is just as critical as what you have to say to them.
- ***Realizing that listening saves time and effort.*** Those

who listen create fewer mistakes, fewer misunderstandings, and fewer false starts.

- ***Understanding that listening to everybody is
  important and worthwhile.*** Look for that something
  you can learn from each and every person you meet.

CHAPTER 6

◆

BECOMING MORE PERSUASIVE

Suppose you take your boss aside to tell him about your great idea for a new software product. It's an off-shoot of your firm's present line, and one you're sure could be easily produced, thus nailing down a profitable niche. You expect him to be as jazzed about it as you are.

Instead, he raises reservations about staff and funding. He voices doubts about timing and market. He questions whether the needed equipment and raw materials are available and, even if they are, whether foreign competitors wouldn't soon catch on and make the same product more cheaply. All in all, his response sounds suspiciously like a brush-off.

Why? Why are so many new ideas a tough sell? Isn't it true, as the old saying goes, that if you invent a better mousetrap, the world will beat a path to your door? No, that's baloney! In fact, it's never been less true. For a variety of reasons.

For starters, people everywhere have become more savvy, skeptical, even cynical. We've all become more jaded about advertising, more suspicious of political claims, and less trusting of those who bring us a message, *any* message—even one that may be in our best interest.

Second, organizations build barriers to change. Change entails risks, and risk conflicts with the desire for control and predictability. Change also requires approval by a lot of people, people with differing needs and interests.

THE ART OF PERSUADING

Third, and most important for this book, many people just aren't skilled at the art of persuading. No matter how brilliant your idea, no matter how technically advanced or economically sound it may be, it'll go nowhere unless you get others to go along with it. And the only way you do that is by persuading them, by communicating clearly why *they* really should want to do what *you* really need done.

John Naisbitt, the futurist author of *Megatrends 2000*, said our high-tech capabilities have outpaced our "high-touch needs." In other words, we spend more and more time learning new technology and less and less time developing the interpersonal skills needed to explain an idea's worth.

As a result, learning to improve our persuasiveness is both easier and harder than it used to be. Easier because we've now got E-mail and voice mail, CD-roms and cellular phones, satellites and skywriting, and a vast array of other tools for communicating. But it's also more difficult in that the deluge of messages and ill-equipped messengers cheapens them all. So nowadays, it's more crucial than ever to hone the skills that heighten our power of persuasion and, in turn, our charisma.

QUICK QUIZ: YOUR PERSUASIVENESS

For each pair of statements below, distribute three points between the two alternatives (A and B), depending on how characteristic of you the statement is. Although some pairs of statements may seem equally true for you, assign more points to the alternative that is more representative of your behavior most of the time.
Examples:

- If A is very characteristic of you and B is very uncharacteristic, write "3" next to A and "0" next to B.
- If A is more characteristic of you than B, write "2" next to A and "1" next to B.
- If B is very characteristic of you and A is very uncharacteristic, write "3" next to B and "0" next to A.

. . . and so on.

1A___I work extra hard when necessary because I want to accomplish my goals and because I enjoy the feeling of success.

1B___I work extra hard when necessary because it's expected of me and I need to set an example.

2A___I get excited trying to persuade others to see my way of thinking.

2B___I believe in "live and let live" and, thus, don't often try hard to get others to come around to my way of thinking.

3A___I use a lot of metaphors, analogies, and anecdotes when I am trying to convince somebody of something.

3B___I think people are persuaded by facts, not by my charm as a storyteller, so I tend to stick to logic and data when I'm trying to convince somebody.

4A___I have a well-defined set of goals for the short, intermediate, and long term.

4B___I have a good, general sense of what I want to accomplish but I rarely express it to myself or others in concrete terms.

5A___I give compliments freely and sincerely.

5B___I'm a little wary of giving too many compliments because it may cheapen their worth or people will think I'm flattering them for my own personal gain.

6A___People often pause thoughtfully when we're speaking and say to me, "That's a very good question."

6B___People rarely comment on my questions.

7A___I often repeat back to another person the gist of what they've just said so that I'm sure I understand the meaning.

7B___Repeating back what's just been said seems unnecessary and time-consuming.

8A___I make it a point to remember others' names and use them in conversation.

8B___I can remember jokes, knots, recipes, and all manner of other minutiae, but I have trouble with names.

9A___When there are multiple, acceptable courses of action, I usually try to see which one most people are comfortable with.

9B___When there are multiple, acceptable courses of action, I try to lead the group toward what I think is the best plan.

10A___When I'm in charge, I put a lot of effort into explaining to others the "why" of what we are doing.

10B___When I'm in charge, I put my priority on getting the job done and, if time permits, explaining the "why" later.

SCORING:

Please add point totals under "A" and enter here: _____

Please add point totals under "B" and enter here: _____

Now let's take a look at how you scored on this segment. If your "A" score is significantly greater than your "B" score (and if you were truly honest!), you are fairly strong in this aspect of charisma. The more lopsided your "A" score, the stronger you are as a persuader. If your "A" score exceeds your "B" by, say, a 2-to-1 margin, your persuasiveness "glass" is far fuller than most.

Conversely, if your "B" score approximates your "A" score, you may have identified an improvement opportunity. And if your "B" score is higher than your "A," that's an indication that you need lots of work in this area.

WE'RE ALL PERSUADERS

Being good at persuading is a major building block of charisma. The truth is, we're all involved in persuasion of some sort every day. If you're in sales, the use of persuasion is pretty obvious: You try to convince others to buy your product or service. But in our social and personal lives, too, there's a more subtle but almost constant use of persuasion as you seek a date, debate politics, try to talk your way out of a parking ticket, decide which video you and a friend will rent, or just make the case that yams, not mashed potatoes, will go better with that Thanksgiving turkey.

But sometimes the process of persuasion is more long term and less obvious than that. Take recycling. Twenty years ago, most people would have thought it was too much of a hassle to keep piles of empty bottles, aluminum cans, or old newspapers in some corner of their home. Today, a great many people recycle, or at least agree that it's a good idea to recycle.

What made us change? A couple decades of persistent persuasion from people in the ecology movement, from companies who care about the environment, and from our friends and neighbors who demonstrate how easy and worthwhile recycling can be. What's in it for us, they said in effect, is that the benefit greatly outweighs the cost, that we can help save the earth's precious resources by just tossing bottles and cans in a couple bins in our garage.

In this chapter, you'll learn some very specific techniques for persuading others to see things your way. And we'll take a look at some of the barriers that often stand in the way of agreement.

THE FOUR-STEP PROCESS

How can you improve your persuasiveness and thus increase your charisma? Well, a starting point is to make sure you and others understand the "need gap." The need gap is the difference between the current situation and the desired situation. Whatever the specifics of a situation, when other people perceive a gap you've cited—a "because"—there's a natural desire to want to fill it. (This is also a component of your "vision," which we'll talk a lot about in a later chapter.)

Here are four steps for determining, and then closing, the need gap and using it as a tool for persuasion. By the way, this tool is universal. It can be applied to large social issues, say, birth control or economic justice, or to more day-to-day challenges such as influencing your customers.

Here's the process:

1. Explore needs and goals
2. Create and select a solution
3. Commit to an action plan
4. Assure success by identifying, monitoring, and measuring results

Sometimes a need gap is obvious. Homeless people need affordable, safe shelter; businesspeople desire freeways that aren't jammed every day at rush hour; and your customer may want new, less expensive technology that completely replaces what he or she is using. But sometimes the gap is not so obvious, and finding it requires exploring the current and desired situations.

1. Explore Needs and Goals

The main way you discover the need gap is by asking questions. Questioning is a very important skill. It makes persuasion easier by getting the person you want to influence involved in discovering the problem (where it "hurts") and being committed to creating the solution (how to make it feel "better").

"Judge a man by his questions rather than by his answers," Voltaire said. Indeed, well-phrased questions are the mark of a skilled persuader. Such queries help people organize their thoughts and feelings.

Thus, you'll get tremendous insight into their needs, motivations, and fears. The answers will smooth the way for the building of a relationship.

OPEN VERSUS CLOSED QUESTIONS

It's best to begin with open questions, the kind that require a narrative for an answer. Such questions can't be answered with a simple yes or no, or a simple fact. These open-ended questions encourage the other person to relax and to think broadly even as they give you a chance to explore.

Proper phrasing makes a big difference in the kind of answer you get. "How's business?" will often get you a pat answer. "Can you tell me a little bit about your business?" is a much better open question.

Similarly, "Are you happy with your current mutual fund?" is not as good as "Would you describe your current personal investment strategy?" "Can you tell me what's important to you in a home-security system?" is likely to be more productive than "So you want a burglar alarm?"

Open questions don't lead the other person in a specific direction but, rather, increase dialogue and show your interest in his or her situation. Once you've gathered information that paints a broad picture, you can use closed questions to get specific facts.

Let's suppose you're thinking about remodeling your home. The first contractor comes to your home and asks a few questions like: "How old is the home?" "What areas do you want to remodel?" "Will you need financing?" "How much equity do you have in the house?" "When do you want the work to start?" Those are all reasonable closed questions that get the contractor some useful information.

Then a second contractor arrives and asks questions like: "Could you tell me a little about your lifestyle?" "Which area of your home is your favorite, and why?" "What do you hope to accomplish by getting this remodeling done?" Then, in addition, he asks the same questions the other contractor did.

Which contractor would you hire? My guess is, all other things being equal, you'd be more influenced by the second builder who started with the open questions, then went to the specific closed questions. He engaged you in an exploration of your need gap, your "because."

Or perhaps you're seeking donations to your university's alumni fund. A good open-ended question to a prospective donor might be: "How do you feel about being an alumna of State?" You can follow this with: "Are you aware of all the good work the alumni fund is doing?" Again, that's an open question followed by a closed question.

THE FUNNEL TECHNIQUE

The "funnel" technique of questioning involves beginning with broad, open questions and then building on those responses by making narrower, more specific queries. As you move down the neck of the funnel, you fill in more and more of the details by asking more pointed questions.

The broad, open questions at the top of the funnel ("What prompted you to look for a new travel agency right now?") are comfortable to answer and give the answerer more freedom. By the time you get to the more specific questions ("How many national trips and international trips, on the average, does your firm book in a month?"), he or she can see where you're going and will be more willing to share information with you. Not only that, most people will experience a higher sense of trust as they reveal information to you gradually.

CLARIFYING, EXPANDING, OR REDIRECTING

It's also important to understand the three primary
directions for questions: clarify, expand, or redirect.

Clarifying questions refer directly to the other
person's remarks. In essence, these questions suggest:
I hear what you're saying but I want to make sure I
know what you mean. Clarifying questions are a form
of feedback, and they reinforce what the person just
said.

Thus, the contractor might say: "Am I correct in
thinking you hope to substantially cut down on your
heating bills with this improvement?" As a fund-raiser,
you might ask: "You're saying that you're proud to be
a university grad but you're not informed about what
the alumni fund is doing these days?" By getting the
person to repeat or affirm a statement, you're
attempting to reinforce his or her need for your service
or cause.

Expanding questions get at more detailed information, such as what the other person's priorities are.
In essence, you're saying: I understand, but tell me
more.

What if the contractor asked, "When this area is
enlarged, what kind of furniture do you plan to put in
here?" That would give him a better idea of your style
preference. You might ask the prospective alumni-fund
donor: "What kinds of activities were you involved in
while you attended the university? What was your
major?" Her answers might suggest a way to elicit her
support.

Redirecting questions are useful for steering the conversation in other directions. In essence, you're saying:
I now have a good grasp of your point of view, so let's
look in another area. These questions can change the
topic, or navigate a difficult exchange toward smoother

waters. If the answer to an expanding question goes on and on, change the topic with a redirecting question.

For example, after hearing all about the furniture, drapery, and carpet choices planned for the remodeled family room, the contractor could gently steer the conversation back toward the overall design. Or, to get feedback on a different issue, you could ask the potential donor this question: "One of the things that the alumni fund is supporting is more research and development for growing crops organically. Since you majored in agriculture, how would that interest you?"

A COLLABORATIVE EXPERIENCE

Using questions makes persuasion more of a collaborative experience. Remember: Increasing your persuasiveness is not an exercise in exerting power *over* people. Some folks may still cling to the old image of using verbal domination to get others to see things their way. But it doesn't work that way in the real world anymore, if it ever did.

Whether you're selling goods, recruiting people to work for political candidates, marshaling support for community causes, or trying to win over people for whatever reason, the emphasis now is on getting that person (1) to acknowledge and share a perceived need (again, a "because") and then (2) to be willing to collaborate with you on solutions.

You'll be a powerful persuader when you can align your vision with the needs, wants, and objectives of other people and get their feedback. Exploring those needs and getting the other person to acknowledge the need gap—the gap between what is and what can be, or the "because"—is the first crucial step.

2. Create and Select a Solution

Usually when you're trying to persuade somebody, there's more than one possible course of action. So in most cases, you'll want to involve the other person in exploring ways to close the need gap. If they're helping create the solution, they'll be far more committed to implementing it than if you unilaterally create the plan and "inflict" your solution on them.

For instance, if you're a real-estate salesperson, you may find a great home that meets a family's living requirements. But it may not meet their criteria for quality of the schools or access to shopping. Or you may be able to meet all the requirements—including schools and shopping—but not at the right price. By collaborating with your customers, you can help solve the problem by getting them to detail their priorities, telling you which of the factors is most critical to *their* plan.

If you're trying to round up volunteers to help out in a poor neighborhood and you're speaking with someone who's already expressed interest, don't *tell* that person what he'll be doing. Instead, *ask* him what he'd feel most comfortable doing and what actions he feels will make the most difference. Helping kids learn to read? Repairing broken windows? Getting inoculations for people at risk?

That way, you'll help establish mutual respect and trust. Trust, says management author and speaker Gordon Shea, is the "miracle ingredient in organizational life—a lubricant that reduces friction, a bonding agent that glues together disparate parts, a catalyst that facilitates action."

The point is, you want to make others feel they have a part in the solution, not feel as if they were coerced or manipulated. Coercing someone into following your suggestions may get you what you want in the short term. But in the long term, you'll lose.

3. Commit to an Action Plan

If yours is a simple sale or other act of persuasion, if a yes or no is all that's required, action is immediate. But if what you're seeking requires several steps or phases, you'll need agreement on how you're going to proceed.

Doctors, for example, often complain that patients don't get well because they don't fully follow the prescription directions. When the patient starts feeling a little better, for example, he or she may stop taking the medicine. Even though the doctor is in charge of the treatment, the patient acts unilaterally and then the doctor gets blamed for the relapse.

Maybe the doctor needs to take time to explain the action of the drugs in relation to the problem. The symptoms of a sore throat can be alleviated in two days with an antibiotic, the physician might say, but the germs may remain for days afterward, and they need to be controlled. Patients who understand the process are much more likely to carry out the plan.

During this step, make sure the other person clearly understands the benefits of implementation. Have them restate the benefits and what it's going to take to get them. For instance, the contractor might encourage the customer to say, "If I invest $10,000 in this remodeling plan now, my house will be worth more when it comes time to sell it, and I'll also save between $500 and $700 a year in heating costs."

An added plus of discussing the follow-up may be that the customer comes up with benefits that the salesperson never thought of. "If I remodel, I can also use the added space for a home office, meaning I no longer will need to rent space downtown and I may be able to take an added deduction on my income taxes."

It's also important to verify that the other person understands the obligations and rewards if he or she takes the action you suggest. If someone has agreed to serve on your nonprofit board, for instance, make sure she knows what's expected of her, how many meetings she'll have to attend, how much fund-raising she'll have to do, and how much cooperation she can expect from the executive director.

Of course, nothing is going to happen if an action plan isn't *agreed upon mutually*. During this step of the persuasion process, there are four "P" barriers that can get in the way of negotiation and agreement: **P**olitics, **P**ostponement, **P**ersonality conflict, and **P**riority.

POLITICS

When you hit the "politics" barrier, it means that agreement will put somebody at odds with somebody else: "If I buy that new car, my wife will kill me." "If I join one more save-the-environment organization, my husband will move my things out into the garden."

Because you're committed to collaboration, you won't ignore such a concern or suggest that it just be ignored. Instead, find out why that third person feels that way. Maybe you can alleviate the concern with new information.

You might say to the prospective car buyer, "Why don't you bring your wife down here on Saturday for a test drive, and we can see what her specific concerns are." To the prospective organization member, you could add, "Here's what we do that's different from all the other environmental groups. Do you think your husband would be supportive of that?" In a situation where agreement is blocked by politics, all you can do is help to create solutions.

POSTPONEMENT

When the other person says, "I need time to think about it," it's very important to find out the real reason for postponement. It can simply be a polite way of saying no. It could be that the person never makes hasty decisions. Or the person may not have all the information he needs and is too embarrassed or too timid to ask for more.

This is where clarifying questions come in handy. "Is anything confusing to you?" "What specifically can I do to help the process along?" "Will you be comparing my offer with someone else's?" Asking questions keeps the door open for agreement.

At the root of this postponement may be personal discomfort. Something about what you're suggesting makes the other person uncomfortable. Maybe they can't even put their finger on it. But chances are their discomfort has to do with risk. You need to find out what they see as the risk.

One technique is to have them list the pros and cons from their point of view. If your suggestion costs money, you can offer a money-back guarantee. If it's membership in an organization, invite them to a meeting with absolutely no pressure to join. If they're put off by a product's unfamiliarity, invite them to try it out.

Provide whatever information you can to give the other person confidence in what you're offering. You can even help them identify the key factors they *should* take into account before agreeing with you.

You can also alleviate personal discomfort and postponement by showing—and this is *very* important!—that
the benefit far outweighs the risk. So remember to
explain clearly the WIIFM factor, or "What's In It For Me?"

PERSONALITY CONFLICT

Even if what you're suggesting or offering seems positive to the other person, they may not like *you*. The
relationship between the two of you is the foundation
of the persuasion process. If that relationship collapses,
so does everything it supports.

One of the most common causes of a personality
conflict is a breakdown in trust. Maybe what you were
offering really didn't have the other person's interest at
heart. Or you made promises you didn't keep. Or
something went wrong, and you made no attempt to
address the problem.

At other times, the personality conflict is simply the
result of different styles of communicating. In Chapter
8, we'll examine in depth how to identify and match
someone's personal style of communication.

PRIORITIES

The other person may think that your idea, product, or
cause is a good one, but it's not among their top ten
priorities. This is when knowing yourself well is very
important. The better you can articulate *why* you value
what you're advocating (the "because" factor again),
the better your chances of striking a chord with the
other person.

When trying to persuade others, you might need to help them articulate what their priorities are—in other words, what they most value. The exploring phase we talked about earlier is the perfect time to investigate the other person's priorities.

Then you can emphasize both the intrinsic value of the idea, product, or cause as well as how it serves the person's priorities.

4. Assure Success by Identifying, Monitoring, and Measuring Results

In California's Silicon Valley, where many of America's most technologically advanced firms compete fiercely, there's an adage: You can't manage what you can't measure. Things change so fast in that high-tech arena, those computer executives say, that it's absolutely critical to get your hands on the numbers and to do so quickly.

There's a lesson in that for the rest of us. While the real secret to long-term influence and power with people is exceeding their expectations, often they don't have a firm idea of what they expect. So you need to help them, first, identify criteria for success. As far as possible, put those goals in quantitative terms—return on investment, say, or number of years a product should last, or the maximum amount of maintenance needed. Offer them *something* concrete.

Second, you need to help them manage their expectations. If they expect too much, you'll fail; if the expectations are too low, anybody could match them. So the secret is helping the person you're influencing try to come up with realistic quantitative expectations.

Finally, you need to measure the promised results and be available if a problem develops. You've got to keep an eye on the results and consult with the other person about how he or she sees them.

What happens if the room addition your company built develops leaks during the first rainy season? What do you do if the elderly woman you recruited to save the trees in the park gets put in jail for joining a protest? In either case, you need to be there, be supportive, and do what's needed to correct the situation.

In other words, the real work of persuading people and maintaining influence with people occurs *after* they say yes. Staying in touch with the people you want to influence, and staying tuned in to their values and needs, are what this fourth stage is all about.

A Quick Review

Let's review the four-step persuasion model: You first explore the needs and goals of the person, getting a broad picture with open questions and then moving to specifics with closed questions. You use Clarifying, Expanding, and Redirecting questions. You work to identify the "need gap."

Then, together, you create options and select solutions, which is the second step. The third step is committing to an action plan, and the fourth step is assuring long-term collaboration by staying close and following up.

And, meanwhile, remember that word: *because*. We all like to have reasons for what we do. When you're attempting to persuade someone, you need to understand your "because"—that is, *your* values—as well as their "because," or what motivates them.

JUMP-STARTING YOUR POWER OF PERSUASION

Persuasion is that all-important ability to get others to do what you want them to do *because* they want to do it. Maybe it takes reasoning, coaxing, explaining, or even a plate of brownies still warm from the oven. But whatever it takes, obviously persuasion is what's needed to make things happen, to take anything from Point A (your idea) to Point B (others helping to advance that idea).

But, again, just ordering people around won't make it happen. In fact, that'll probably have the opposite effect over the long run. "The three keys to persuasion," says motivational trainer Peter Lowe, "are: Establish rapport. Establish rapport. Establish rapport."

To build that rapport, you need to cultivate behaviors that will make people trust you and make them feel it's in their best interest to follow your lead. Here, then, are some ideas, big and small, for making yourself more persuasive:

1. *Ask yourself: What do I really want?* Sure, we all want security, happiness, health, love, and fulfilling work. Digging a little deeper, we might find further shared values, such as recognition, power, freedom, and serving others.

But what's unique to you? What do you think about alone at three in the morning? What really resonates within your soul? What would you, in a perfect world and freed of family, fiscal, or geographic constraints, most like to be doing?

Think about these questions as a means of searching for your great "because."

2. *Shift your focus to others.* There's an old story of a young lady who was taken to dinner one evening by William Gladstone and then the following evening by Benjamin Disraeli, both eminent British statesmen in the late nineteenth century. "When I left the dining room after sitting next to Mr. Gladstone, I thought he was the cleverest man in England," she said. "But after sitting next to Mr. Disraeli, I thought I was the cleverest woman in England."

Disraeli obviously had a knack for making the other person the center of his universe, if only for the evening. This may sound manipulative, but if you practice attentiveness to others, you'll find it does wonders for both of you. They'll enjoy it; so will you. And together you'll accomplish much more.

So make a conscious effort to think of others' wants and needs before your own. Later we'll talk in detail about what differing personalities specifically seek. But meanwhile, start training your mind not to focus automatically on what separates you from the other person. Rather, figure out what unites you, and how you can build upon that base. Soon such empathy will become a habit. A very good habit.

3. *Be quick to compliment.* This is an ancient art fallen into disuse. A really good, honest compliment

shows that you appreciate the person you admire. There is no shortage of critics. But there is a dearth of people who say nice things when they genuinely feel them.

"Feedback," says Ken Blanchard, co-author of *The One-Minute Manager* and other motivational books, "is the breakfast of champions." People want and need to know how they're doing.

Be on the lookout for positive acts and attitudes worth noting. You'll convince the other person that you care—and you'll convince yourself as well.

4. ***Train yourself to remember other people's names.*** The sweetest sound, it's said, is that of your own name being spoken. And calling others by name is an important first step toward building rapport and, thus, persuasion.

Yet names of strangers tend to flit through most of our heads with lightning-like speed. Roger Dawson, in his book *13 Secrets of Power Persuasion*, gives numerous techniques for overcoming this problem. One of the best: When you shake hands with a new person, note the color of his or her eyes. That forces you to make eye contact and, after a while, will also send a signal to your brain to store that person's name in your short-term memory. Use the name soon afterwards, and you'll have a lock on it. Try it!

5. ***Empower others.*** Skillful persuaders send out the message, spoken or unspoken, that they appreciate others' abilities. For example, Minnesota Mining & Manufacturing (3M), the $15-billion-a-year firm famed for its innovation, encourages technical people to spend 15 percent of their time on projects of their own choosing. It also gives employees grants of up to $50,000

to pay for prototypes or testing of their ideas and allows employees to form companies among themselves to develop and market a new product. At the firm, where videotape, Scotch tape, Post-it notes, and literally tens of thousands of other products were invented, leaders still utter—and follow—the maxims of William McKnight, its legendary leader for half a century: "Listen to anybody with an idea." . . . "Encourage experimental doodling." . . . and "If you put fences around people, you get sheep; give people the room they need."

6. *Try to arouse positive emotion.* Persuasive leaders often use drama or play to stir up positive emotions. So try a playful gesture, such as a light tap on the shoulder to emphasize a job well done. Or set up an awards ceremony so good works will be publicly noted. Or write a short note of appreciation. In other words, do something nice and unexpected.

Another way to stoke positive emotion is by trying to make tasks exciting. Be enthusiastic. Talk up the job. Emphasize its importance. Use stories and metaphors, which often are more motivating than reason or statistics or duty alone.

7. *Take a clue from your audience.* Think of whom you're trying to persuade, and what's the most comfortable way for them to receive messages. Elaina Zuker, author of *The Seven Secrets of Influence*, tells of trying to get the editor of a large magazine to use some of Zuker's audio cassettes as an educational tool for the magazine's readers. She sent over the tapes, but weeks went by without a response.

The editor then asked if Zuker could send written summaries of the tapes. At first, Zuker mildly protested, telling the editor she already had the tapes—all she had to do was listen to them. *Finally*, Zuker says, she got the picture: The magazine editor, not surprisingly, was more at ease with reading something than hearing it. In other words, she "saw" in print.

Zuker sent over the tape transcripts, and within two days they had a deal. "This was a great lesson for me," Zuker wrote. "There was nothing wrong with the content of what I presented. The audio form was simply the wrong medium to use when dealing with a visual person."

In Chapter 8, I'll also show how different personality types often prefer to receive material in different ways. That'll further help you match your message to the receiver.

8. *Hone your sense of humor.* While being wheeled into the operating room after being shot by a would-be assassin, the ever-persuasive President Ronald Reagan got a chuckle when he wisecracked, "I hope the doctor is a Republican." We may not all be so cool in a crisis, but we can all profit by not taking ourselves too seriously.

Humor is an infinitely variable commodity, on the part of both the sender and the receiver. Witness the range of comics from, say, The Three Stooges to Mort Sahl or audiences as disparate as Shriners and anthropologists.

My suggestions for improving your sense of humor: *First*, find out what your strong suit is, humor-wise. Ask a friend who'll be honest with you. *Second*, research your audience. Find out who they are, what's made them laugh previously. *Third*, work on your timing. Try out your best lines on your family, friends, and associates. *Fourth*, if humor hasn't previously been in your repertoire, proceed slowly. It's better to use humor sparingly than to be remembered as a buffoon or insensitive.

Fifth, sprinkle your humor throughout your talk, not just at the beginning or end. *Sixth*, make it relevant to the subject, not just a funny line you paste onto your speech for laughs. And, *last*, remember that some of the best stories are those you tell on yourself. A little mild self-deprecation can go a long way toward making your audience feel at ease with you.

Such conversational first aid not only makes the other person or group more persuadable, it helps you both keep your perspective. Humor not only can be an icebreaker, but if the going is tough, to those in the trenches it can also be an affirmation of dignity, a declaration of your collective faith in the ultimate triumph.

9. *Practice being a better questioner.* Most of us get sloppy when asking questions. Perhaps an acquaintance has just told us of a bizarre or difficult occurrence, and we reply rotely, "Isn't that something?"

Yes, it obviously *was* something—and something important, too, or this person wouldn't have told us about it. It'd be better to take his lead and follow up by asking, "How does that make you feel?" or "Have you ever experienced anything else like that?" or "How could that be handled differently in the future?" or "I wonder what lessons we can take from that?"

Then you'd have the basis for building conversation and rapport, making him or her—and probably yourself—feel better.

10. *Keep your perspective.* Yes, persuasion is a critical component of charisma. Yes, you feel strongly about the points you're making. Yes, you're as earnest as a person can possibly be. And, yes, you're using the four-step process.

But the world won't stop spinning if today you can't convince someone of the evils of off-track betting or the merits of environmentalism, if they won't buy the camcorder, or decline to make a tax-deductible contribution to your organization.

Despite the undeniable correctness of your point of view, lighten up. Tomorrow's another day—and another opportunity to persuade.

CHAPTER 7

◆————————

USING SPACE AND TIME TO YOUR ADVANTAGE

Human beings are territorial creatures, whether we're talking about space or time. Almost every day, you and I are affected by how we and others use these two powerful, nonverbal communication tools.

Let's say:

> It's the second day of a two-day seminar, and you walk into the conference room with its scores of chairs, and someone has the nerve to be sitting in *your* seat, the one you had occupied only yesterday! Of course, you know you have no claim on that chair. And, what's more, who the heck cares where anybody sits? A week from now you'll have a tough time recalling the topic, let alone who sat where. But still, you feel a slight pang of pain that someone took "your" seat!

> Or you show up promptly for your 2:45 P.M. doctor's appointment. But after flipping through old magazines for fifteen minutes,

you start glaring at the clock and thinking dark thoughts about how this doctor probably purposely schedules patients too close together just to maximize income. Doesn't he know you have a job? What, you ask yourself, would happen if you charged *him* at his rate for the time of yours he wastes?

Or you arrive early at the movies, snag some popcorn and sodas, and settle down in a couple of middle seats in the center of the theater. As the lights go down and the previews begin, your spouse visits the rest room. You put a sweater over the empty chair and casually drape one arm over it, too, so there can be no mistaking that the seat's occupied. But that doesn't keep dozens of latecomers from inquiring, as the movie is about to begin, "Is that seat taken?" Arrghhh! Of course it is. Do they actually think a choice center seat in the middle wouldn't be taken by now? And can't they read the signals? And who do they think they are, anyway, coming in so late and disrupting everything?

Use of space and time, indeed, sends important signals. In this chapter, you'll learn how to communicate your message more skillfully and how to understand the signals others send. We'll see how to use space and time to repair communication that sometimes gets off track—as well as how to create the greatest advantage for yourself while giving the most comfort to others.

For example, if you violate others' physical comfort zone by, say, standing too close to them or sitting in the wrong place or touching them when they think you shouldn't, you may offend them and cause tension. Similarly, if you abuse another person's sense of time— by being too late or too early, for example, or by leaving too quickly or staying too long—you can negatively affect results.

Conversely, you can enhance your charisma by staying flexible and being aware of the time and spatial needs of others. By deciding where someone should sit when they enter your office, for instance, and by limiting what distractions can intrude on your meeting, you can actively set a tone and send out a message. And, as you've already learned, the message you send out has a lot to do with your charisma.

QUICK QUIZ: YOUR USE OF SPACE AND TIME

For each pair of statements below, distribute three points between the two alternatives (A and B), depending on how characteristic of you the statement is. Although some pairs of statements may seem equally true for you, assign more points to the alternative that is more representative of your behavior most of the time.

Examples:

• If A is very characteristic of you and B is very uncharacteristic, write "3" next to A and "0" next to B.
• If A is more characteristic of you than B, write "2" next to A and "1" next to B.
• If B is very characteristic of you and A is very uncharacteristic, write "3" next to B and "0" next to A.

. . . and so on.

1A___I'm well known as a stickler for punctuality.

1B___I'm sometimes late but usually have a good reason or make up for my tardiness by almost always having something of consequence to say when I arrive.

2A___When visitors come to my office, I choose where they and I will sit based on the nature of the conversation.

2B___I don't believe where we sit has much importance compared to what we say.

3A___If I did a pie chart showing how I use my working hours, probably the biggest piece of the pie would represent productive tasks that further my goals.

3B___If I did such a chart, probably the biggest piece of the pie would represent the "odds and ends" that necessarily consume the day of almost any busy person.

4A___When I enter a setting with strangers—such as a cocktail party or classroom—I tend to sit or stand next to someone immediately and start a conversation with him or her.

4B___When I enter an unfamiliar setting, I prefer to sit or stand off by myself at first until I can scope out the situation.

5A___When I meet people in my office, I usually hold all calls, ignore E-mail, put paperwork aside, and devote my full attention to the visitor.

5B___When I have visitors, especially routine ones, I often maximize my productivity by tending to some other easily handled matters at the same time.

6A___If I am to make the best impression, I think my desk and office should look organized.

6B___I expect to be judged on the quality of my work, not on how my office or desk looks.

7A___If I'm late, I make it a point to explain why.

7B___People are interested in results, not excuses. So I prefer just to get down to work.

8A___If I visit another's office or even a cubicle, I don't walk in unannounced or uninvited.

8B___If good working relationships are in place, there ought to be little concern about who's invited where.

9A___A meeting site ought to be chosen with an eye to what's most comfortable for all, physically and psychologically.

9B___Agendas, not sites, are what make good meetings.

10A___If the person I'm talking to is sitting, or is significantly shorter than I, it's wise to approximate eye-level contact.

10B___ Some people are tall, some short; some sit, some stand. Who cares so long as the quality and content of the dialogue are good?

SCORING:

Please add point totals under "A" and enter here: _____

Please add point totals under "B" and enter here: _____

Now let's take a look at how you scored on this segment. If your "A" score is significantly greater than your "B" score (and if you were truly honest!), you are fairly strong in this aspect of charisma. The more lopsided your "A" score, the stronger you are in managing your space and time. If your "A" score exceeds your "B" by, say, a 2-to-1 margin, your space and time "glass" is far fuller than most.

Conversely, if your "B" score approximates your "A" score, you may have identified an improvement opportunity. And if your "B" score is higher than your "A," that's an indication that you need lots of work in this area.

USING SPACE TO YOUR ADVANTAGE

People value their personal territory and privacy. I once was talking to a man and I noticed that if I took a small step forward, he took one backward. Then I made the mistake of touching him on the arm. He froze and stared at my hand. I learned quickly that the amount of space he needed for comfort was much wider than mine.

Anthropologist Edward T. Hall coined the term *proxemics* to describe the study of the spatial separation people naturally maintain. You can use space to your advantage, or disadvantage, in communicating with others. To help you make the most of proxemics, let's look at *territory*, *environment*, and *the four zones of interpersonal space*.

Territory

Recognizing that other people feel territorial will help you gain their respect. When you're conscious of what others have defined as their territory, you give them a sense of control. Violating their boundaries will cause anger, while respecting them may gain you points.

An obvious example: A co-worker has her door closed, and you walk into her office without knocking. Tension skyrockets, and her trust in you—and probably her enthusiasm for whatever it is you're advocating—plummets. In fact, studies have shown that if you're talking to someone and inadvertently violate his personal space, he may not say anything to you directly, but internally he may be so upset that he doesn't hear a word you say.

Similar reactions might occur if you sat in the co-worker's chair, used her pen without permission, or grabbed her personal appointment book to check a date for a future meeting. You may also have experienced something along these lines if you've ever walked into your children's bedroom unannounced. So if you're attempting to build rapport with someone, don't violate his or her territory, even if you're the boss.

Trust is based on honoring a person's territory and promoting mutual respect. So to increase trust, get in the habit of knocking before entering a colleague's office, even if it's for a quick, casual meeting. Similarly, if the meeting is going to last a few minutes, allow the colleague to take the lead by suggesting where you should sit and whether the door to his or her office ought to be open or closed.

Environment

Architects have long been aware that the design, color, and placement of objects in an environment can help or hinder communications. Dr. Anthony Athos, in *Interpersonal Behavior*, has identified several commonly accepted rules about the use of space in work environments. You or I may not like or agree with each of these rules. But being aware of them can add power and clarity to your communications.

1. More Is Better than Less

Space is a limited resource, so the more space people are assigned as personal territory, the more valuable and important they're assumed to be. Normally, then, the higher a person climbs in any organization, the larger his or her office is.

In addition, because windows also provide the illusion of greater space, you'll usually find higher-status people occupying larger offices with nicer views while lower-status employees occupy the inside offices without desirable views.

What does this mean for you? If you've got the bigger office, then people automatically assume you're in the superior position. That can be a plus, if you're dealing with a competitor in a potentially adversarial relationship like, say, a negotiation. But, as is more common, if you're trying to promote trust in a critical meeting with a colleague, you might want to meet in his or her office, or perhaps arrange your office furniture in a way to suggest a more intimate space, as I'll explain below.

2. Private Is Better than Public

Another way of communicating status is by having personal territory that can be closed off from the sight and sound of others. In most organizations, moving from an open, public space to a private office is a signal of increased importance.

Offices are territories with unmovable boundaries such as walls and doors, which come under the heading of "fixed features." But you can also carve out territory with "semifixed features," too.

Typists, for instance, are usually situated in a common "pool" area. But executive secretaries often have fixed-feature territories separated by partitions, giving them some privacy. The manager of the typists and secretaries probably has a private office with a door and other fixed-feature characteristics.

If you have private space, you can choose to confer status on underlings by inviting them in for a closed-door meeting, even if the topic is nonsensitive. Thus, the employee will likely be seen as privileged because he or she may have access to important information that's not available to others.

3. HIGHER IS BETTER THAN LOWER

Executive offices often are on the upper floors while the work areas are on lower ones. Thus, it's often a sign of elevated status to occupy higher territory than others.

So if you're on the upper floor and choose to project authority, you might invite others up to your roost. But if you're seeking to build trust and informality in a more casual setting, you might meet at their offices or cubicles or at a conference room on a lower floor.

That's not a rule that's cut in stone, though. Mark McCormack, author of *What They Didn't Teach You at Harvard Business School* and other books, recommends always trying to meet on your turf. First of all, he says, you have more control there. Second, meeting there brings with it a subtle sense of "invasion" by the other party. "Simply by being polite and making the other person feel comfortable," McCormack reasons, "you can diffuse that tension and earn a certain amount of confidence and trust even before the meeting begins."

Further, if you remain standing over others when they're seated, you may appear to be talking down to them. The same is true if you're taller than the other person. In general, then, to build rapport, it's best to try to communicate at roughly the same eye level.

4. BIG AND EXPENSIVE IS BETTER THAN SMALL AND CHEAP

The size and expense of objects in a territory also sends a message and can influence others positively or negatively. In general, top executives may have desks the size of small yachts and original artwork on their walls while posters suffice in the employee lounge. Similarly, the company may lease a luxury car for the president while lesser employees are offered economy models from the car pool for business purposes.

Again, by choosing your accoutrements, you send out a message, positive or negative. If being respected is important in this situation, the bigger, more expensive objects may be the way to go. But say the company is enduring tough times and you want to project a spartan image; being ostentatious could backfire.

One firm spent about $1 million refurbishing its executive suite just as the company entered its worst-ever economic downturn, replete with wage freezes and layoffs. The opulent executive offices embittered some employees who saw them as a symbol of the disparity between the "haves" and "have-nots."

So the point is, in some situations going big and expensive suggests admirable class and sophistication, especially when all, or most, employees bask in the feeling of success. But there are other times and other corporate cultures where you don't want to give the impression that you're overly materialistic.

5. NEAR IS BETTER THAN FAR

Being assigned space close to the top executive is usually a sign of status because, if for no other reason, it allows for more exposure and chance for being noticed. This can be a mixed blessing, though, because such scrutiny can bring added pressure.

Another example is the way parking spaces are assigned. The lowest-ranked employees may not even have a parking area assigned, while upper-level managers and executives may have personalized, private spaces close to the front door.

Again, if you seek an image of informality and equality, you'll downplay such spatial signals. On the other hand, you may want to use such perks to suggest added respect and status for the major decision-makers, thus motivating others to aspire to those ranks.

USING TERRITORY POSITIVELY

Knowing all this, how can you use territory to build rapport? Well, as we've seen, you can arrange for meetings in locations that make participants feel comfortable and important. Let's say that managers of the Marketing Department and the Production Department are going to meet. A neutral location—a conference room on another floor, for example—might be best to avoid territorial problems. Also, flexible seating should be encouraged to allow attendees to establish their own semifixed territories.

Other meeting pointers about space:

- If a meeting is to be one on one, again, intimacy might be helped by a neutral place. If it's an informal superior-subordinate meeting, it might even occur in the subordinate's office.
- When two people meet casually about a subject on which they feel comfortable—both with one another and with the topic—a corner-to-corner seating arrangement (at right angles to one another) is often

preferred. This allows for unlimited eye contact and maximum use of other nonverbal signals, such as gestures.

- More formal or competitive situations—such as negotiating, delivering a reprimand, or presenting a fitness report—probably call for an across-the-table/desk arrangement. This provides the safety of a barrier and allows close monitoring of nonverbal clues.

The Four Zones of Interpersonal Space

Another way we communicate is by how we treat the air space around us. We assume that this is our personal territory, much like a private "air bubble," and we may resent others entering it unless they're invited. For example, have you ever sat next to a stranger on an airplane or in a movie theater and jockeyed for the single armrest between you? Or felt uneasy when a stranger in an elevator stands too close?

The size of these private bubbles varies from culture to culture, from gender to gender, and from one personality style to another (as will be discussed in a later chapter). But there are general guidelines involving distance and touching, and understanding them will help add to your charisma.

For instance, research has revealed that adult Americans have four basic zones of interaction:

- *Intimate Zone:* from actual contact to about two feet.

  This is touching range, such as you might use when you hug, pat someone on the back, let a friend cry on your shoulder, or read a report looking over someone's shoulder.

- *Personal Zone:* from two to four feet.

  We use this for discussions intended to be private, such as sharing a confidence.

- *Social Zone:* from four feet to twelve feet.

  This is comfortable when you don't mind others overhearing, say, a sales presentation or a very brief, casual exchange.

- *Public Zone:* more than twelve feet.

  This distance is used to establish formality and control when speaking before a group. Note that when speakers want to retain that authority (say, at a press conference), they usually stay behind the podium and directly in front of the group. But if they seek to establish an open, informal dialogue (like a trainer, or a motivational speaker, or a boss trying to convey camaraderie), they'll normally move away from the podium and sometimes even down into the audience.

How you feel about people entering these different zones depends upon who you are and who they are. You might feel uncomfortable and resentful if a business acquaintance entered your Intimate or Personal Zone during a conversation. But if the person were your spouse, you'd probably feel good.

Manager/employee relationships usually begin in the Social Zone of four to twelve feet, although they often move to the Personal Zone as time passes and trust is built.

There's a natural tendency to stand farther away from powerful, influential people. Watch the next time you're at a big company meeting, and you'll likely see the smaller honchos standing farther from the big honchos than from each other. When that starts happening to *you*, you'll know you're doing something right!

THE ROLE OF GENDER

Gender also plays a role. Most of us—no surprise!—like to be closer to people of the opposite sex than to those of our own gender. But females are capable of tolerating less space between each other than males are when they interact with other males.

Research shows that male employees permit female supervisors to get closer to them than male supervisors. But female employees display no difference in the space they permit between themselves and their supervisors, whether female or male.

The role of touching in the workplace is increasingly emotion-filled. While touching can underscore much of what we wish to communicate to colleagues—friendliness, consolation, or excitement, for example—it can easily send the wrong signal and be interpreted as sexual harassment.

And it's not just men touching women that can lead to misunderstandings. One manager had to restrain a young female intern—seemingly from a large, loving family where touching was the norm—from routinely hugging colleagues, even her bosses, beginning the very first day she was on the job. Workers of both genders complained, and the manager gently told her she must stop; the intern seemed totally unaware of having made others uncomfortable.

CULTURAL DIFFERENCES

Cultural differences often come into play with regard to touching. People can generally be classified into two major categories: "contact" and "noncontact." Contact people sometimes view noncontact people as cold and impolite. On the other hand, noncontact people may feel that contact people are aggressive or even rude.

According to Edward T. Hall's *The Hidden Dimension*, some peoples—such as Arabs, Latin Americans, and Italians—normally use a lot of contact in their conversations. On the other hand, North Americans and northern Europeans typify the non-contact group and employ smaller amounts of touching. Of course, because so many cultures are represented in North America, there *are* significant numbers of Americans who are "contact" people.

When a proxemic violation such as unwanted touching occurs, noncontact people may have a feeling that something's not right, but can't pinpoint exactly what's wrong. They'll center their attention on why the other person isn't behaving in the "proper" manner. They may even begin to focus on themselves, becoming self-conscious. In either case, attention shifts to the *behavior* and away from the *conversation* at hand. This interferes with effective communication.

A commonly used example is that of a South American and a North American businessman at a cocktail party. For the South American, the appropriate zone for interaction may be Personal to Intimate and could include frequent touching to make a point. The stereotypical North American needs about twice as much space to be in his comfortable Social Zone.

The South American may step closer and the North American backward in a strange proxemic dance, until both of them give up the relationship as a lost cause because of the other's "cold" or "pushy" attitude. Both of them fail to see what Hall calls "the hidden dimension" in their behavior.

TACTICS FOR REDUCING TENSION

So to maximize your charisma, how should you deal with the private-"air-bubble" issue? How can you use space to help you increase rapport? How do you protect your space as well as not invade that of others?

Initially, when meeting a new person, you'll get best rapport by establishing a social distance (four to twelve feet) and then slowly moving, as the relationship develops, to a personal distance (two to four feet). Be careful not to move too fast—that increases tension—or too slowly, because that makes you seem cold and aloof.

If you feel threatened, you can simply move away until the intruder is in a more acceptable zone. Other tactics to widen the zone include avoiding eye contact or placing an object between you and the other person, such as a footstool, your leg, or an elbow.

For your part, be alert to any negative reaction your sense of distance may cause. It's natural for many of us to lean forward, talk faster, and gesture more when we really get into an idea. In our effort to generate enthusiasm, we may even stand up and move toward the other person. If that's your natural inclination, fine. It'll certainly suggest your exuberance and—if the other person is a "contact" person—you'll probably enhance your charisma.

But if they're not, you may seem pushy and threatening. So, again, remain alert to what effect you're having and don't get too carried away until you're able to see how you're being received.

Whatever the distance, body language also needs to be appropriate during the conversation. Standing or leaning over someone who is seated does convey power, but it can be intimidating for the sitting person. On the other hand, leaning back and appearing too casual can foster a feeling of superiority or lack of caring, again creating a possible negative reaction.

In a good interactive relationship, both parties respect space and use it effectively. The net result is more attention, more trust, better communication, and a better chance for a successful relationship.

USING TIME TO YOUR ADVANTAGE

Like space, time is a resource. But unlike other resources, time must be spent as soon as you receive it. There are ways to increase the amount of money we make or the space we occupy, but nothing we can do will change the amount of time allotted to us. Each of us has the same 24 hours, or 1,440 minutes a day, to work with.

Your use of time is an expressive language. Whom you give time to, how much you give, and when you give it convey important messages. Treat other people's time as if it is as precious as yours, and you'll increase your charisma. Waste their time—especially if they're time-conscious individuals—and you'll squander their respect.

When your boss keeps you waiting, for example, he sends the message that your time isn't as valuable as his. When a co-worker is chronically late for a meeting, she implies that company time isn't valuable. And if someone arrives an hour early for a meeting, he communicates that he thinks his own time isn't worth much.

Generally speaking, in our Western culture, inaccuracy with time creates a bad impression. So the boss who values his influence will make every effort to see you at the scheduled time, and the co-worker will be prompt for the meeting, neither noticeably late nor too early.

TIME AS A SIGN OF CARING

Someone who's frequently late sends the message that he or she doesn't care. That may not be true, but that's the message, and it may injure his or her chances for rapport. So our accuracy with time often broadcasts a signal about our priorities, though it may not be the signal we intend.

Because time is viewed as such a scarce resource, whom we choose to spend it with is often taken as a signal of whom we care about. You can build more productive relationships by simply stating out loud why you spend your time as you do. Let's say you're a manager who absolutely must spend some time returning a series of important phone calls. You might tell your employees: "Hey, I'm going to be out of pocket this morning on an important matter I can't dodge. But I should be free by early afternoon, and the door to my office will be open, as usual. Thanks for understanding." That way, those you usually talk to won't feel shunned.

Time also can be used to demonstrate how we feel about others in terms of their status and power. If the president of the company calls a junior manager to her office for a meeting, the manager will probably arrive before the appointed time. Because of the difference in status, most subordinates would probably feel that any inconvenience in waiting ought to be theirs. The president's time is implicitly regarded as worth more and, therefore, is not to be wasted.

But nonetheless, the longer people are kept waiting, the worse they're likely to feel. Imagine a middle manager summoned to a meeting with the president at 1:00 P.M. She arrives at a respectful 12:50, and remains comfortable until 1:10, when she asks the secretary to remind the president that she's there. If the secretary checks and then conveys that the president will be right with her, the manager will probably remain comfortable until around 1:25.

By 1:45, however, she's likely to be quite angry and to assume that the president doesn't really care about seeing her. If the president then has the manager sent in and proceeds directly to the business at hand without offering an explanation, the manager will probably feel hurt. This may affect the meeting and the relationship negatively.

But, on the other hand, if the president apologizes and shares some inside information while explaining why he's running late, the manager is more apt to get over it because, after all, the boss's time is very important.

Human beings like reasons for things. If you have a good reason for being late, you have a chance to do some damage control. A legitimate excuse and some reassurance can help the other person feel better. And the longer a person is kept waiting, the more reassurance is required to neutralize the irritation.

LIKES AND DISLIKES

We're constantly broadcasting to the world what we like and what we dislike by how we use our time. The way we spend our money tells others what we value, and so does the way we spend our time. We signal our priorities by choosing to go to our child's Little League game rather than working overtime. Likewise, deciding to spend time perfecting the budget rather than listening to an employee's problem sends a message. While some demands on our time are out of our control, we need to be alert to what messages we send by our use of time.

Alec Mackenzie, author of *The Time Trap*, a classic work on time management, says that "time management" is really a misnomer. "For we cannot manage time. We can only manage ourselves in relation to time. . . . We cannot choose whether to spend it, but only how." Among the biggest time wasters, Mackenzie says, are management by crisis, telephone interruptions, poor planning, attempting too much, and drop-in visitors as well as procrastination and an inability to say no.

WHAT TIME SIGNALS ARE YOU SENDING?

If you are chronically disorganized or late, you may be a liability to your organization and an embarrassment to your friends and associates. Such behavior could call your dependability into question. You may need a crash course in time management, the bedrocks of which are establishing goals and priorities and then sticking to them.

Improving your time management can boost your productivity, help you achieve your goals, reduce stress, and attain a better balance between your work and your personal life. Willingness to work long hours is noble but, if long hours become routine, often they are nonproductive. Anyone's ability to do good work drops off sharply after eight hours or so.

So the aim of getting a better handle on your use of time isn't just to get more work done. Rather, it's twofold: You'll get a great reputation for *reliability*, which will boost your charisma, and you'll have more time for *fun*, which will make your life richer.

JUMP-STARTING YOUR EFFECTIVE USE OF TERRITORY

By recognizing how you use your own space and time—and how you react to others' use of those two resources—you can become a more skillful communicator. Remember, how you honor or violate another person's proxemic zones will affect the amount of tension or trust between you.

Likewise, your use of time sends out either positive or negative signals. If the signals are that you value the other person's time, your chances of gaining influence rise dramatically and, with them, the likelihood of cooperation and productivity.

Here, then, are some ideas—some new, some repeated for emphasis—about how you might use space and time to increase your charisma:

1. *Find out exactly where your time goes.* If you think you're too busy to figure out exactly where your

time goes, then you're precisely the person who should compile a detailed time log.

So for at least three days, or better yet for a week, keep close track of how you spend your days—how many total minutes on important and unimportant phone calls, how many minutes studying papers or restudying papers you've already read, how much time socializing, planning, daydreaming, being interrupted, and making significant headway.

Then figure out where you're wasting your time in relation to your priorities. Being too busy to come to grips with time management is like putting off getting your roof repaired because it's the rainy season.

2. *Try delaying procrastination.* Studies show that about 20 percent of American adults habitually procrastinate and, as a result, suffer personal or professional consequences. When they don't finish projects on time, they often undercut their charisma and send the wrong kind of messages to their colleagues.

So fight procrastinating by:

- *Crying uncle.* The biggest fear for many procrastinators is telling the boss they can't do everything. But it's far better for everybody if you do a few things well rather than a lot of things poorly.
- *Setting deadlines.* Even if a project comes without a deadline, give it one. You'll be amazed at how much work you can get done when you're up against a cutoff. Remember how much you accomplished that Thursday when you wanted to take off the next day for a long weekend?
- *Derailing digressions.* Take note of the wasted effort in stopping then restarting tasks. Learning to concentrate on one thing at a time may take a great deal of discipline. But if you commit now to finishing a

job—or at least an identifiable chunk of it—before putting it down, you'll be on the way to developing a habit that will pay off well for you in the future.

- *Rewarding yourself.* Best of all, give yourself an "Attaboy!" when you finish a project on time. Maybe it's just an ice cream cone or a walk around the block on a sunny day, but still it's positive reinforcement.

3. *Signal your time shifts.* What if you had a friend who for years called you about once a week, and then, suddenly, stopped calling? You'd wonder whether you had said or done something to offend. Or whether he or she has lost your number. Or found a new friend he liked better.

The point is, because we tend to read messages into time changes, it's important to signal others when our time priorities change. If your boss tells you that your work has reached such a high level that he's going to spend more time training newer staffers, wouldn't that be more reassuring than if he just started avoiding you?

Show sensitivity to others by telling them if you're going to make a change. This will build more productive relationships and keep others from making the wrong assumptions about your priorities.

4. *Learn to say no.* This is one of the strongest time-management tools, Mackenzie believes, and a way to avoid overload, overtime, and stress. Because of the need to please, the fear of offending, or other emotion-laden reasons, we sometimes undercut our own priorities and undervalue our own time. So we say yes first and regret it later as we let others squander our time.

"We have to prevent others from wasting our time," says Mark McCormack, a globe-trotting executive I quoted earlier in this chapter. "This calls for alertness, assertiveness and tact."

One way to do this is to figure out how long a given conversation or meeting should take and then allot it neither more nor less time than it deserves. Or you can practice counting to ten before responding to a request for your time—and if the answer must be no, suggest other ways, or other people, to meet the requester's need. Above all, keep your own priorities firmly in mind.

5. *Start using your office proactively as a tool.* Close the door when you invite someone in, even if it's just for an informal chat. They'll feel more important, and you ward off most interruptions. Speaking of interruptions, don't answer your telephone, reply to E-mail, sign expense vouchers, or attend to other such tasks when you have someone with you. It's rude and sends the message that you don't care what the other person is saying.

Similarly, how you arrange your office furniture affects your visitor. If you sit in your chair behind your desk, there's a barrier between you and them, signaling a short superior-subordinate interaction. If you want a more informal, relaxed, one-on-one atmosphere, sit closer to the visitor, without the barrier of a desk.

Also, if people seem to need to lean over or around you as they work with you, rethink whether your furniture, equipment, and desk items are functionally placed. Visitors should be able to reach them without invading your sense of space. So rearrange the items to reinforce the personal space you need—or remove them altogether to create a more open, hospitable space for joint efforts.

6. *Scope out your space.* Is a clean desk a sign of a sick mind? Or is it just the opposite? More importantly,

what does your space say about you? That you control the job, or that the job controls you?

Whether you work in a private office or a general space, your work area makes a statement. Maybe it says "Organized" or "Busy"—or maybe it says "Help!" The point is, people notice. And if you're often losing things or missing appointments, if co-workers smirk and ask about the severity of the recent "earthquake" when they visit your office, you're needlessly hobbling your charisma.

If that sounds familiar, it may be time to:

- Get tough with your in-basket. If you don't need something, toss it.
- Take a course or read a book on how to become more organized.
- Start keeping a "To Do" list and commit to getting on top of tasks.
- Buy one of those pocket-size electronic organizers that sounds an alarm when appointments or deadlines are looming.
- Hire a consultant, or ask a friend for help.

7. *Learn to manage interruptions.* Managers are especially torn by trying to be both accessible and productive. They want to be modern, sensitive bosses who will hear out customer complaints and employee problems—but they also have planning to do, projects to complete, paperwork to handle, goals to meet, and higher-ups to satisfy.

Here are some techniques for striking a balance:

- The telephone, Alec Mackenzie suggests, is one of the biggest time wasters. He gives several strategies for dealing with interrupting phone calls, such as call screening, voice mail, and the like. But perhaps the simplest solution is to put a three-minute egg-timer on your desk. When the sand runs out, you know to call a halt diplomatically to all but the most critical of calls.

- An open-door policy is fine, but it can destroy your efficiency if taken too far. Roger Dawson, in *13 Secrets of Power Performance*, offers numerous ways to lessen drop-in visitors. One, arrange your office so you aren't readily visible and thus a target for people passing by with time on their hands. Another, set a block of time—usually early in the workday or near the end—when employees do a lot of socializing, and make that your official "closed-door" period when you can hole up and not feel guilty.

- Go to lunch at an odd hour, say 11 A.M. or 1 P.M. Not only, Dawson believes, will you get a better table and service at the restaurant, you'll be working when everyone else is out to lunch. Thus, your productivity will soar.

8. *Avoid talking down.* Be sure to keep in mind the difference in height—yours and the person you'd like to influence—when starting any kind of a lengthy conversation. If the person is sitting at a workstation, pull up a chair and approximate eye-level contact.

Or if he or she walks into your office, either invite your visitor to sit down (if it's likely to be a lengthy discussion), or stand up yourself if it's just a quick conversation. Either way, you'll promote rapport.

9. *Give good meeting.* Meetings aren't supposed to be, as one office wag said, "a practical alternative to working." In fact, if you plan both the time and space, meetings can be productive as well as a means of promoting relationships.

Space. Try to hold meetings in an attractive location so participants will feel comfortable and important. If they enjoy their surroundings, they'll probably have a more positive attitude toward the discussion. A neutral location avoids the territorial problems of meeting on someone else's turf. Movable seating allows participants to establish their own semifixed territories and spatial arrangements.

Time. Meetings have been described as "a place where you keep the minutes and lose the hours." To avoid this, it's always wise to have an agenda and a time limit. Tell everyone when you expect the meeting to end. That'll help everyone stay on track and get everything done.

10. *Honor space and time in the "virtual office," too.* With so much work now being done via E-mail, videoconferencing, and other electronic formats, it's easy to forget how many of the same tenets of time and space apply. For instance, to maximize your charisma, be sure to start or enter teleconferences promptly, not late. Further, if you E-mail a request to a colleague or subordinate, show respect for his or her time by telling them how urgently you need the answer, or whether a reply is needed at all.

While a video conference eliminates some of the nuances of where you're sitting or standing vis-à-vis the other participants, don't forget that they still may be watching you on the screen. Be careful not to abuse the comfort that comes with distance by picking your nose, using unseemly facial expressions or gestures, or yawning or seeming distracted when others are talking.

Keep in mind, too, that in electronic communication, the visual cues—such as obvious mood and posture—

are usually absent. But trust is just as important as in a face-to-face meeting. As a result, you need to be particularly sensitive and respectful about what the other person may be thinking or feeling.

Such thoughts or feelings would be automatically communicated if you were in the same room together. But because you're not, because you may just be sending and receiving typed messages on a computer screen, be especially mindful of your "table manners." So think how others will likely receive your message before you launch it into cyberspace. And if there's any doubt as to what the other person may be feeling, tread softly.

CHAPTER 8

◆

MAXIMIZING YOUR ADAPTABILITY

> The sleek auto—really a sculpture on wheels—spins smoothly through the tight curves of a spectacularly scenic road. Below, surf crashes. Above, peaks soar. And in the car, the driver's face ignites in pride and pleasure at the sheer joy of being at the wheel of a machine that looks so grand and performs so well.

You've shown that video a thousand times, never failing to take pride in the Brigadier, *your* Brigadier: strikingly handsome, reliable, and comfortable, yet competitively priced. Happy Brigadier owners, including yourself, are many and loyal.

You've studied everything about the Brigadier, from its advanced independent-suspension system to its state-of-the-art stereo down to the last lug nut on its titanium-alloy wheels. Further, you, as a salesperson, take pains to look sharp—neither flashy nor stuffy, but competent. And having read every book on sales and gone to every skills-building seminar, you *are* an able and experienced salesperson.

So why don't you sell more cars?

The way you see it, with such a great product and—let's not be modest, now!—such talent and diligence, you ought to be able to sell to almost any serious prospect. But, in truth, you just don't mesh with a number of prospective buyers.

You sense it in your gut almost the second they walk in. There's something about them—or is it something about you?—that sends out radarlike pings that return this unspoken message: "Not a chance, bub."

Despite a good product and a strong presentation, you know these people will walk away and not return. They may vaguely suggest that the car is too expensive or not precisely the right color. Or they may say nothing at all.

But from your years in the business you know the real reason: You somehow didn't connect with them, didn't build that all-important bond. You never quite got on their wavelength. As a result, they didn't relate to you, aren't about to relate to you, and probably wouldn't accept an award-winning Brigadier from *you* if the car were free.

Why?

LIKE SNOWFLAKES

The reason is that, like snowflakes, we're all different. There's no other person in the world exactly like me, or exactly like you. That definitely makes life more interesting—but also more difficult at times.

At the car agency, for example, a quick summary

emphasizing bottom-line results might be a sure-fire technique for one prospect. For another, knowing that he or she will be the first in the neighborhood to own a stylish new Brigadier could be a far better sales pitch. Yet another customer might want to establish trust and rapport with you before buying, while still another wouldn't care if you were their "friend" but would definitely want time to study hard data about reliability and resale value.

Why so many different approaches? And how do you tell which will work best with which customer? The answers are rooted in the fact that each of us has a preferred way of relating to others. It's called our "personality style," or behavioral style. Understanding and adapting to those styles is an important key to charisma—and a boost to your chances of success in any field.

The truth is, most of us don't try very hard to understand others. We scratch our heads in puzzlement at those who are unlike us, and then we bumble along, pretty much resigned to the fact that a lot of people out there are just, well, different, odd—or even weird. So we ignore them, or deal with them as little as possible, often to our detriment.

But when we fail to understand others, when we just assume they ought to be more like us, we create tension and discomfort—otherwise known as "personality conflicts." You can reduce or eliminate those conflicts by learning to understand behavioral styles, including your own.

Daniel Goleman, in his best-selling book, *Emotional Intelligence*, said that "much evidence exists that people who are emotionally adept—who know and manage their own feelings well, and who read and deal effectively with other people's feelings" have an advantage in all of life's arenas. Further, they're "more likely to be content and effective in their lives, mastering the habits of mind that foster their own productivity."

Thus, you'll lessen tension—and likely help your career, improve productivity, increase sales, foster better customer relations, maximize your strengths, and, in general, enjoy a fuller, more successful life—if you learn to identify those styles and adapt to them. And you'll go a long way toward becoming more charismatic.

QUICK QUIZ: ADAPTING TO OTHERS

For each pair of statements below, distribute three points between the two alternatives (A and B), depending on how characteristic of you the statement is. Although some pairs of statements may seem equally true for you, assign more points to the alternative that is more representative of your behavior most of the time.

Examples:

• If A is very characteristic of you and B is very uncharacteristic, write "3" next to A and "0" next to B.
• If A is more characteristic of you than B, write "2" next to A and "1" next to B.
• If B is very characteristic of you and A is very uncharacteristic, write "3" next to B and "0" next to A.

. . . and so on.

1A___I often play a game—such as cards, croquet, or volleyball—without much thought as to who wins.

1B___I rarely undertake any activity without trying to do my very best.

2A___I can listen to a radio talk show and strongly disagree with the host or a caller without getting upset or changing the station.

2B___I get irritated at some of the wrongheadedness I hear on those shows and much prefer something more in line with my own values.

3A___I frequently will step outside my comfort zone and take a risk—whether physical, social, moral, or financial.

3B___I know myself pretty well, am comfortable with my likes and dislikes, and see little reason to take unnecessary chances.

4A___I often will admit to others that I made a mistake or that we are at odds on some point.

4B___Though I sometimes err and do disagree with others, I think it's better to forge ahead rather than spending time and effort rehashing the past.

5A___When I negotiate, I strive to understand all parties' concerns and work to help others achieve their goals as well as to accomplish my own.

5B___When I negotiate, my first obligation is to assure the achievement of my own goals.

6A___Given enough time to figure them out, I can get along with almost anyone.

6B___Sometimes two people are just like oil and water, unable to find compatibility no matter how hard each tries.

7A___If I meet a person who's fast-paced, say, compared to my more contemplative approach, I naturally speed up in order to try to bridge the gulf between us.

7B___Faced with such a situation, I'd just continue to act as I always do and hope our approaches wouldn't become an obstacle.

8A___Under the skin, we're all essentially engaged in similar psychological and physical struggles.

8B___I'm a unique individual, with different needs and wants than others.

9A___I work hard, and largely successfully, at getting along with everyone.

9B___Try as I might, there are certain people I just can't stand.

10A___I'm pretty flexible on any issue that doesn't diminish my integrity.

10B___Sometimes when you know you're right, you just have to hang in there, come hell or high water.

SCORING:

Please add point totals under "A" and enter here: _____

Please add point totals under "B" and enter here: _____

Now let's take a look at how you scored on this segment. If your "A" score is significantly greater than your "B" score (and if you were truly honest!), you are fairly strong in this aspect of charisma. The more lopsided your "A" score, the stronger you are in adaptability. If your "A" score exceeds your "B" by, say, a 2-to-1 margin, your adaptability "glass" is far fuller than most.

Conversely, if your "B" score approximates your "A" score, you may have identified an improvement opportunity. And if the "B" score is higher than your "A," that's an indication that you need lots of work in this area.

FROM THE ANCIENT TO THE MODERN

For centuries, people have been fascinated with each other's differences. Beginning with the early astrologers and the ancient Greeks, there have been many attempts to understand people by dividing personalities into categories. A breakthrough came in the 1920s when psychiatrist Carl Jung wrote his famous book, *Psychological Types*, in which he described four behavioral styles: the Intuitor, the Thinker, the Feeler, and the Sensor. Jung believed that each of us carries all four attributes, but we tend to rely on one or two over the others.

Today, there are dozens of models of behavioral differences. Some are highly complicated, involving sixteen or more types and subtypes. But most have a common thread—a basic grouping of behavior into four categories. Those categories mirror our habits and our ways of looking at the world. And we signal our category, or style, by how we shake hands or organize our office, whether we're chatty or curt on the phone, the way we approach tasks, how we embrace or resist change, the speed and rhythm of our speech, and a myriad of other ways.

This chapter will show you how to spot the basic clues that each personality style sends out—as well as how to deal with people of that persuasion. We're going to use a very simple model that's been validated in research with hundreds of thousands of people. It's a powerful guide that's simple, practical, accurate, easy to use, and easy to remember.

With this knowledge, you can take control of your compatibility with others. You'll improve communication and be able to build rapport with anyone. Further, it'll help you understand yourself better. The result should be a terrific shot in the arm for your charisma.

THE NEW GOLDEN RULE

You remember The Golden Rule: "Do unto others as you would have them do unto you"? Well, that's a wonderful axiom, as far as it goes. But not everybody wants to be treated the same way you do!

I think the real intent of the Golden Rule is to treat others the way *they* would like to be treated. Hence, I've come up with what I think is a newer, more sensitive version of The Golden Rule—or what I call **The Platinum Rule**™:

> "DO UNTO OTHERS AS *THEY'D* LIKE
> DONE UNTO THEM."

In fact, along with behavioral scientist Dr. Michael J. O'Connor, I wrote a book that examined the personality styles much more deeply. *The Platinum Rule: Discover the Four Basic Business Personalities—And How They Can Lead You to Success* (Warner Books, 1996) describes four core behavioral, or personality, types:

The Dominant Directors

These are forceful, take-charge people. Their impatience—and sometimes their insensitivity—may make you wince. Neither shy nor subtle, they'll probably point out if your socks don't quite match or if a picture on your wall isn't perfectly straight.

But there's no denying they're leaders: direct, decisive, determined—and often domineering. Driven by an inner need to get results, they're firm in their relationships with others, and more concerned with outcomes than egos.

Almost always in a hurry (they love car phones and E-mail), always working toward a goal, always strong and opinionated, Directors stir up dust and create energy wherever they go. They're highly competitive people. For example, one Director I know took up the piano in middle age and was making good progress until he discovered the complicated piece he'd been laboring over had been written by Beethoven at age five. The Director, realizing he'd never match that kind of genius, immediately gave up the piano for some other hobby where he'd have a shot at being the best.

Directors are good administrators and managers, working hard, quickly, and impressively by themselves. In short, they do whatever it takes to get things done, even if that means stepping on toes. When others can't keep up, Directors may let it be known that they view those people as weak or incompetent. Despite being driven, Directors rarely get ulcers; they *give* ulcers to other people!

If they were generals (and many good generals are Directors), their straight-on approach to attacking the enemy would be: **Ready . . . Aim . . . Fire! Fire! Fire!**

The Interacting Socializers

The friendly, enthusiastic Socializers want to be in the middle of the action, whatever and wherever it is. They're fast-paced people who thrive on admiration, acknowledgment, and applause. Basically, their highest priority is to have fun and enjoy life.

Flashy and popular, they enjoy being trendsetters, sporting the latest fashions, spouting the hippest lingo, tossing around the newest ideas. So while also fast-paced like the Directors, they're much more people-oriented than task-oriented.

They love to talk, and while strong on fresh concepts, they're usually weak on execution. Energetic and spirited, they seek to influence others in an optimistic, friendly way and focus on positive outcomes. Their primary weaknesses are getting involved in too many things, being impatient, and, because they're easily bored, having a short attention span.

For instance, I know one Socializer boss whose staff has dubbed her method of leadership "drive-by management." That's because, like a drive-by shooting, it involves brief, irrational fireworks without much follow-up.

As our hypothetical general on the battlefield, the Socializer's orders would probably go like this: **Ready** . . . **Fire! Fire! Fire!** . . . **Aim.**

The Steady Relaters

Relaters are the teddy bears of the human zoo, and people feel good just being with them. They're the most people-oriented of all of the four styles. So having close, friendly relationships is one of their highest priorities.

One Relater I know can be gone for just a day and return to find as many as a dozen messages on her answering machine, including a number from her former in-laws, who keep in touch regularly despite the divorce. Most of the callers just want to say hello or find a willing ear. That's because Relaters, usually good listeners who are extremely supportive, have tremendous counseling skills. As a result, they have strong networks of friends and acquaintances—and are terrific parents!

Rather easygoing and slow-paced, Relaters believe in self-control and tend to follow the rules. They generally reserve their opinion and are usually patient and diplomatic. However, Relaters tend to drag their feet when it comes to change, preferring routine ways of doing things. They're usually quite willing, though, to be good, pleasant followers and let others lead. They especially enjoy belonging to what they see as a good team.

The low-key Relaters dislike interpersonal conflict so much that they sometimes are too timid and may say what they think other people want to hear. So they can be unassertive, overly sensitive, and easily bullied.

As generals, their orders might be along the lines of **Ready-Ready-Ready ... Aim ... Fire!**

The Cautious Thinkers

Like the Director, the Thinker is a results-oriented problem solver. But he or she seeks results in a quieter, more low-key way that is less likely to ruffle feathers.

More introverted than Directors, Thinkers are analytical, persistent, independent, and well organized. Also unlike Directors, they don't like to call attention to themselves, preferring to work alone quietly and painstakingly—so much so that they're often seen as aloof, picky, and critical.

Thinkers very much want to be accurate and correct. Thus, they're cautious, not impulsive. They sometimes take so long collecting data that they're slow to reach a decision. But if given a strict deadline, they rarely miss it.

They love order. One Thinker I know, for example, alphabetizes his extensive library and lays out his office wardrobe a week in advance.

They're noncontact people who are not fond of huggers and touchers, or loud people. The Thinker shuns razzmatazz, preferring, say, a cool handshake or a brief telephone call to a raucous greeting or an attention-getting performance.

Thus, emotions often take a back seat. Thinkers fear uncontrolled feelings and irrational acts, either their own or those of others. So they seek to avoid embarrassment by exerting tight control over themselves. Detail-oriented and somewhat rigid, they are irritated by surprises or glitches.

If they were generals, their command probably would be: **Aim-Aim-Aim ... Ready ... Fire!**

A QUICK REVIEW

So do you recognize yourself? Or those around you? Can you identify the types you're drawn to—or maybe those that drive you up a wall? And do you see which type is best?

Well, the answer to that last question is: No! None is better than the others, although some styles may work better in certain situations. For example, you could certainly see a Socializer as a cruise ship social director. But would you want a Socializer as your CPA?

The point is, all types have their strengths and weaknesses. Directors are great leaders who get results but can be ham-handed when it comes to dealing with other human beings sensitively; Socializers, though warm and energizing, often are disastrous with detail. Relaters are calm and kind but can easily get stuck in a rut. Thinkers are precise, dependable analysts but often are about as jolly as an IRS auditor.

But, let's face it, we need all four. If we were all Directors, there'd be plenty of leaders but no followers.

If each of us were a Socializer, life might indeed be a cabaret—but would anything get done on time? If everyone were a Relater, the world would be a chummy place, but would lack a certain drive, and if we all were Thinkers, perfection might be plentiful but warmth and camaraderie might be in short supply.

The more familiar you become with other styles, the better you'll be able to "speak their language." For instance, you generally wouldn't suggest to a Director that you meet over a long, slow lunch. You're better off suggesting a quick "power" breakfast at 7:15 A.M. And you wouldn't open a business conversation with a Relater by reciting your thirteen-point plan and supporting data. A Relater would rather get to know you first.

LEARNING TO SPOT THE STYLES

With a little study, you'll soon be able to spot Directors, Socializers, Relaters, and Thinkers as easily as you can tell a bungalow from an apartment house, or a sports car from a station wagon. The simplest way to start sorting out the behavioral types is, first, by just listening to *how much* a person talks.

Extroverts—no surprise here!—talk more. Two of our personality types—the Director and the Socializer—are outgoing, fast-paced extroverts. Of course, as we've learned, they're outgoing in different ways: One's a commanding presence and the other's more of a natural showman, an entertainer. But neither is bashful. They're both emphatic, energetic talkers. So for starters, if you meet someone, especially for the first time, and they come on strong, they're likely either a Director or a Socializer. That's your first clue.

Conversely, if they're quiet and soft-spoken, they're probably a Relater or a Thinker. Those two types, more naturally introverted, are not so quick to assert themselves or reveal what they're really thinking. So right away, if you can peg someone as assertive and talky, or low-key and reserved, you're already halfway there!

A second major sign is *what* people say and *how* they say it: their words, and the pace and priority of those words. Directors, as we've seen, are aggressive, results-oriented people for whom accomplishing tasks is very important. You can expect them to speak quickly, strongly. They tend to listen less and talk more, usually making strong statements rather than asking questions.

Be alert for these kinds of statements from a Director:

"Tell him I want to talk to him ASAP."

"Let's get this settled right now."

"What's the bottom line?"

"Cut to the chase: What are the options?"

That's a Director: strong and talkative, but in a way that moves the discussion firmly ahead toward his or her most prized goals: Solutions. Progress. Winning.

Now the Socializer is also an outgoing, verbal person. But he or she's more sociable, playful, and fun. They're more inclined toward people than tasks. In fact, Socializers are usually downright chatty—but their words will have a different ring from those of the Director. The Socializer, who is seldom authoritarian, will be more likely to include you in the conversation and be more vague about results.

You could expect a Socializer to tell more stories and jokes and say things such as:

"Hey! Here's an idea! Whaddaya think?"

"Spare me the details. Just give me the drift."

"I feel this is the way to go to . . ."

"Tell me what you think about . . ."

Again, if the person you meet is assertive and talkative, he or she is probably a Director or a Socializer. You can determine that almost instantly. Then listen to his or her words. If the talk is about tasks and results—words like *output, competition, success,* or *triumph*—it's likely a Director you're hearing. A Socializer will talk more about people and ideas and include words like *feeling, impression, team,* and *concepts*.

THE FLIP SIDE

Okay, but let's say this person you meet isn't talkative. The person doesn't start off acting as if he or she has known you for years or as if he or she has been put in charge. In fact, when you meet the person, he or she is quietly pleasant and low-key. So what you likely have is a Relater or a Thinker. They're quieter and more introverted, listening more and talking less.

When they do speak, it's often with questions rather than direct statements about their own thoughts or feelings. They're the kind of people who probably wouldn't plunge into a crowded room but instead would take a few minutes to size up the goings-on from the sidelines. Observing that, you can eliminate Director or Socializer. But how do you distinguish between Relater and Thinker? Well, again, listen to *what* they say.

Relaters are friendly, sensitive people, maybe a bit indecisive or even acquiescent. They like to ask the opinion of others and wouldn't think of forcing their views on someone else. They like stability and being accepted. So you'll probably hear them say things like:

"I'd like to go kind of slow on this. Is that okay?"

"Can we do this together until I get a feel for it?"

"I'll help if I can, but I don't want sole responsibility."

"How do you really feel about this?"

Thinkers, while also reserved and slower paced, are not as concerned with being part of the team and avoiding risk at all costs. They're very independent people. They're much more into getting things done than Relaters but in a much more understated way than Directors.

Here are the kinds of phrases you might hear from a Thinker:

"Now, let's look at this logically."

"Is that the right thing to do? Can we justify that?"

"Let's take this first step. Then we can decide on Step Two."

"Have we touched all the bases?"

So, again, if the person you meet is relatively reserved and low-key, he or she is likely a Relater or a Thinker. That's a call you can make almost instantaneously.

Then listen to the person. If he or she is warm, friendly, and talks a lot about people, feelings, and togetherness, you've probably found a Relater. A Thinker, while also reserved, has a bit of a sharper edge. He or she wants to solve problems, get things done, make progress—but all in a calm, nonobtrusive, orderly way.

PUTTING THIS INTO PRACTICE

Now, knowing all this, how are you going to sell more Brigadiers? For starters, you need to know that customers don't buy because they're made to understand the details of the product or service. They buy when *they* feel understood. So the successful salesperson shows customers that he or she understands them by giving them what they expect—and more. But more what?

Now that you understand behavioral styles, you know that "more" for the Director customer is more *control*. But the Socializer cries out for more *recognition* and *excitement*. The Relater wants more *support*, and the Thinker more *logic* and *caution*. The best salespeople customize their approach and follow-through.

(And—importantly—though I'm using a sales situation as my main example, these same principles apply in every relationship every day, whether you're at work, home, or wherever. In "Jump-Starting Your Compatibility" at the end of this chapter, I'll show how you can apply the same concepts to other situations.)

But, meanwhile, let's say you spy a customer checking out the latest Brigadier model on the showroom floor. You go over and engage her in conversation, keeping a sharp eye and ear for signs of her personality style. She's a serious woman, strong, forceful, opinionated, rather blunt. She asks the questions, doesn't tell you much about herself, seems intent on controlling the conversation. A Director, you deduce.

So what do you do? Tell her a funny story so she'll be dazzled by your wit? Come on strong like an old school chum? Of course not. Remember, Directors are task oriented, and while they want to have confidence in the people they deal with, they don't need to develop a bond with them. So skip the jokes and the banter and get to the point. Offer solutions that'll provide the results she wants. Don't oversell or waste her time. Spell out the options, backing each one up with evidence.

Be cool. Directors put a low priority on feelings, attitude, and advice, so don't hustle them—just give them the facts in practical terms and you'll stand a much better chance of making the sale. Above all else, be efficient and competent.

On the other hand, you may run into another customer with a colorful outfit and a gift of gab and judge him to be a Socializer. Remember, he isn't into facts or logic as much as a hope that the Brigadier will help him stand out. Also, Socializers think the sales process should be enjoyable, so your funny story might be more appropriate here. But, most of all, Socializers need approval and may want to become your friend before being sold. Be enthusiastic, keep the paperwork and follow-up to a minimum, and stress, if you honestly can, the change and innovation that the new Brigadier embodies.

So show that you like and admire them, and be prepared to listen to their personal feelings and experiences. Socializers think out loud and love to brainstorm, to engage in verbal give-and-take. Above all else, be interested in Socializers and let them talk!

A Relater, meanwhile, also wants to trust a salesperson before making a purchase. But Relaters are rarely in a hurry and likely will be turned off by pushy, aggressive salespeople. Relaters respond well to sincere, friendly attention and to those who listen and are sensitive to their needs.

Keep in mind that the Relater has a low tolerance for conflict, and avoids risk or radical change whenever possible. So tell them what to expect, step by step, if they were to buy the car. And you may need to give them time to think things through. When you're attempting to sell something to a Relater, concentrate on security, harmony, and concrete benefits.

The Thinker, in contrast, isn't as interested in friendly attention as he is in detailed information about how this car will work for him. Cautious by nature, Thinkers want to reduce risk. So anything you can offer along the lines of a guarantee or a trial period will help cinch the sale.

Like the Relater, the Thinker will be turned off by salespeople who seem to be too direct or too enthusiastic. Thinkers distrust hype in any form. When you approach Thinkers, remember that they want data, not chitchat. Be thorough and well prepared and make sure your presentation matches their organized, thoughtful approach. And Thinkers like to be right, so allow them time for deliberation and analysis to find the "best" or "correct" answer. You mustn't rush a Thinker.

Demystifying Compatibility

So, you see, compatibility, or the lack of it, is not such a mystery. Both rapport and tension are rather predictable, once you know what to look for. The point is: *Everybody is easy to please, if you know how.*

Adjusting your style to the styles of others is called adaptability. Highly adaptable people aren't prisoners of their own styles. They're good at getting in sync with others because they use their brains as they were intended to be used: to determine what types of behavior are most appropriate in what situations.

Thus, a highly adaptive Director would not merely be controlling but, if the situation required, would be outgoing like a Socializer, or sensitive like a Relater, or cautious like a Thinker. Likewise, highly adaptive Socializers, Relaters, and Thinkers see when they need to escape their comfort zones and adapt in the interest of getting the job done. The antidote to most personality conflict is just that obvious. Cultivate a style that's adaptable. Give your full attention to the other person and seek to cooperate, not confront.

This adaptability is the key to successful relationships of all sorts. Some of us adapt easily, naturally; others must work at it because lifelong habits of competition and conflict are not altered overnight. But it's do-able *if* you're committed, *if* you use both your head and your heart. Adaptability comes from understanding people's inner needs—and then working to meet them. Do so, and you'll find that *your* needs will get met, too.

MAXIMIZING YOUR ADAPTABILITY

Adjusting Pace and Priority

You can get rid of much tension in a relationship if you start by simply adjusting your *speed* of doing things. Then alter, if needed, your priority—that is, whether you emphasize *task* or *relationship*.

For example, Directors and Socializers are fast-paced. But to deal better with Relaters and Thinkers, they need to allow decisions to be made slowly and more privately. So in dealing with Relaters and Thinkers, try to be more relaxed. Ask their opinions and find ways to acknowledge and incorporate their views into the dialogue. Follow their lead rather than attempting to take control. Make it a point to listen more than you speak, and when you do speak, don't interrupt, challenge, or push the process along faster than they want it to go. Be tactful about any disagreement.

Similarly, if you're a Relater or Thinker seeking to work with a fast-paced person, you need to pick up the pace. Initiate conversations, give recommendations, avoid beating around the bush. Maintain eye contact, use your firmest handshake, speak strongly and confidently.

As for priority, Relaters and Socializers naturally emphasize relationships and feelings instead of the tasks and results favored by Directors and Thinkers. So to deal better with a Director or Thinker, you'll want to stress results. Get right to it: Talk about the bottom line, use lots of facts, and logic. If possible, prepare an agenda and stick to it. Keep your meeting focused and short. Downplay your natural ebullience.

Conversely, if you're a Director or a Thinker, put the relationship first when dealing with the other types. Seek to share your feelings. Open up and let the Socializer or Relater know you. Show an interest in him or her: their job, family, or hobbies, for example. And then use that knowledge in the future to personalize your dealings with the Socializer or Relater. Seek to speak in a friendly, informal way. Be flexible with your time, tolerating digressions, such as stories and anecdotes.

Not Imitation

Adapting doesn't mean imitating another person's style or pretending to be someone you're not. But it *does* mean being willing and able to bend a bit if that's what it takes to make a better relationship. It's a way to work better with a specific person or a certain situation. It means thinking before you act. It means not just doing or saying the first thing that comes to your mind.

The truth is: You do it all the time. Don't you show a different side of yourself when you go to the boss's house for dinner than when you go to a friend's place for a game of cards? Don't you act differently at a ball game than you do at a business meeting? And do you behave the same at an art museum as you do at a St. Patrick's Day party? Of course not.

You adapt because you sense that a different type of behavior is called for if you're to be successful and to be accepted. And you're right. The key point is: You can sharpen that skill of knowing when and how to adapt. You can learn to adapt to all kinds of people and situations. As a result, you can find success and acceptance you never dreamed of.

Let me give you another simple illustration of making a decision based on someone else's preferred style. Let's say that you and the person you want to influence have agreed to meet after work. He wants you to decide where. If you've determined this person's a Director, you'll want to keep in mind that he generally feels pressed for time and isn't into long-winded chats. Your best bet, then, might be to choose a quiet café that's nearby and has good, quick service.

If he's a Socializer, you can probably pick a more casual and lively place. Maybe a spot with a happy hour and free hors d'oeuvres, or an ice cream parlor with an upbeat, fun ambience.

If he's a Relater, you want a smaller, more intimate environment. These folks often have a fondness for tradition and the past, so a meeting place with historical pictures on its walls would be appropriate. You might even suggest a park or botanical garden for your get-together.

If he's a Thinker, you'd better play it safe—at least the first time. Pick a place where serious business is regularly conducted. Make sure the prices are reasonable. And verify that it won't be too crowded.

Some Last Words of Advice

By choosing how you act, you can encourage others to respond more positively. Thus, you can enlarge your charisma or, if you will, your personal magnetism. This works not only for adults in the workplace but for people of all ages in all of life's other arenas—home, school, sports, shopping, you name it! Anywhere you seek better relationships, you can, with practice, transform your encounters into positive experiences. By dealing with people as they want to be dealt with, you'll make them more comfortable with you—and heighten the chances for a win-win relationship that'll enhance you both.

Being the best person you can be by treating people the way *they* want to be treated pays off enormously.

And not just in making a sale or negotiating a deal. Rather, a further big dividend comes in creating a web of rich relationships that makes for a fuller life.

Thus, **The Platinum Rule**, distilled to its essence, equates to respect for others. It's an attempt to break down the them-versus-us mentality and concentrate on the "us." It's a potent tool for helping build your charisma by meeting the other person's needs *and* your own.

JUMP-STARTING YOUR COMPATIBILITY

Knowledge is power. You should use wisely your powerful new knowledge of the behavioral styles. Employ **The Platinum Rule** to understand yourself and others, to improve yourself, and to build bridges to those around you. What it's all about is being sensitive to others. So a person who truly practices adaptability is more tactful, reasonable, understanding, and nonjudgmental.

Here are some added tips to help you build rapport:

1. *Reach out and touch someone.* Think of a "difficult" person with whom you'd like to communicate better. Which of the four styles best describes that person? (He or she probably has a different personality style from yours.) But think for a moment: What motivates that person? For a Dominant Director, it's control; for an Interacting Socializer, recognition; for a Steady Relater, camaraderie; and for a Cautious Thinker, analysis.

In each case, there's something in their background that propelled them in that direction. Don't condemn—

understand! And then ask yourself: What can I do that will reinforce what this person needs most?

2. ***Don't overdo it.*** Remember that not everyone knows—or cares—about the behavioral styles. And they probably don't want to think they're being categorized by you, either.

So I suggest that you show some restraint. You're probably asking for trouble if you attempt to jazz up the office party by doing an instant, colorful analysis of the Big Boss's personality style.

3. ***Don't be too quick to judge.*** Being able to recognize the styles is important, but adapting to them is even more vital. So be careful about judging someone's style too quickly—"Oh, he's a Cautious Thinker, and I don't get along with Cautious Thinkers, so I won't waste my time with him"—and making irrevocable decisions based on your perceived compatibility. Your knowledge of the styles should expand your relationships, not limit them. So don't use **The Platinum Rule** to stereotype or pigeonhole others.

4. ***Use self-knowledge as an insight, not an excuse.*** Knowing your style is a wonderful way to improve yourself. For perhaps the first time, you'll see your strengths and weaknesses as others do. But don't use this as a crutch to justify unacceptable behavior, thinking thoughts like, "I'm a Dominant Director. So I'm naturally impatient and domineering." Or "It's okay if I don't follow up because I'm an Interacting Socializer."

5. ***Work on improving your adaptability.*** Relationships, like money, must be managed. With attention and practice, you can learn to handle relationships in a

way that allows everyone to win. For starters, whatever your style, here are some simple actions that'll help improve your compatibility:

Socializers Can ...
Control time and emotions
Try to be more objective
Follow up on promises, tasks
Focus on the job at hand

Thinkers Can ...
Openly show concern and appreciation of others
Make timely decisions
Use policies as guidelines, not laws
Collaborate by seeking common ground

Relaters Can ...
Say no occasionally
Take some risks
Avoid undue modesty
Accept logical changes

Directors Can ...
Project a more relaxed image by pacing themselves
Become more open, patient listeners
Give verbal compliments
Act less hastily, more cautiously

6. *Learn to motivate by style.* Whenever you face a task—at the office or in the home, with colleagues, friends, or family members—it's likely that a big chunk of your effort involves attempting to motivate others. You can use your knowledge of **The Platinum Rule** to explain the challenge in a way that each type can best relate to.

Here's how you might inspire each:

Dominant Directors: Be straightforward: Here's what's wrong, here's how it came about, here's how it's likely to affect us. "So," you might say to them, "let's get working on ways to conquer this problem."

Give the Director some measure of control that will inspire him or her to further achievement. "You're resourceful," you might say. "I don't have to tell you how to do your job. The point is: The decision's been made. Now it's up to us to show how we can perform."

Interacting Socializers: Explain that while meeting this challenge may be difficult, it'll also distinguish those who do. Remind them, if it's true, that you've come to count on them; cite their awards and accomplishments. Repeat the good things others may have said to you about their work.

Explain how their status and visibility could be raised. "This is a rare opportunity, not a setback. Every set of eyes in the place is going to be watching us. It's our chance to shine. And we *can* do it!"

Steady Relaters: The Relater is particularly cool to change, any change. So support his or her reluctance. Tell the Relater warmly, calmly that this problem just comes with the territory. Stress that it's not going to affect the teamwork we've developed, and that, *together*, we can surmount this hurdle.

Promise to sit down with them later to see what impact it's had on them. And if it's had a negative effect, pledge to work with them to remedy that.

Cautious Thinkers: He or she will want to know in more detail the reasons behind the problem or the challenge. So be organized, thorough, and precise in your explanation. Provide documentation, and explain as fully as you can any new procedures or plan.

"Here are the facts," you might say. "So our best bet is to fully understand the problem and then logically figure out how to attack it."

7. ***Tailor your criticism by style.*** Telling someone
they need to improve is difficult but often necessary at
work and at home. The key is to tell them in a way that
doesn't put them on the defensive, that appeals most
positively to their personality style.

Some possible approaches:

Dominant Directors: Stress the result wanted and, as
far as possible, let them come up with ways to achieve
it. Set a time for them to get back to you with a
progress report. For example, you might say, "Our goal
is to totally eliminate billing errors. If anybody can do
it, we can. Let's make this a major push, and let's get
started right now."

Interacting Socializers: Don't be vague. Specify
exactly what the problem is and what behavior is
required. Have the Socializer repeat the agreed-upon
changes back to you so there's no chance of miscommunication. "We're being scrutinized by the big bosses
on how well we deal with this problem; our reputation
as a department is at stake. So I need you to get cracking
on this plan. Top priority. I'll send you a memo underscoring what we've talked about here. Any questions?"

Steady Relaters: Focus on performance, not personality. They're sensitive, so go out of your way to
explain that there's nothing wrong with them personally—and stress empathy. "You can understand, I'm
sure, what it'd be like to be one of our customers and
suffer this problem. We both want to keep these customers happy and our team morale high. So please
help me in trying to eliminate these errors."

Cautious Thinkers: Be specific. Say precisely what's
being done wrong, outline the steps for correcting it,

and set a deadline for completion. Plan another meeting in a week or two to see how those steps are working and whether midcourse corrections are needed. "We're probably not going to lick this thing all at once," you might say. "But let's get a good remedial plan on line—and then we can take it from there."

8. *Improve your family ties.* "You can pick your friends," the old saying goes, "but you can't pick your relatives." That's true, and it's likely there's somebody in your family who's difficult for you to deal with.

Let's briefly examine what to expect from each of the four styles, family-wise, and then suggest how differing styles can become more compatible.

Dominant Directors: These types often run into difficulty in family situations because they consider themselves results specialists—but families are often more about controlling damage than achieving results. Directors are usually flops as emotional backstops, and their tendency to make every decision a negotiation can wear on other family members.

Directors are also likely to have lots of firm ideas about how other family members can perform better. If others get upset at such constructive criticism, the Director will probably withdraw rather than have to wrestle with the emotional fallout.

If you're a Director, you can better adapt to your family by:

- Not always taking charge. Let someone else make some of the choices.
- Learning to laugh at family foibles. It's just a home, after all, not a contest for cumulative points.
- Keeping silent sometimes. Let others see if they can

figure out the answers, which, of course, you may already know.

• Verbalizing and enjoying positive emotions. Make an effort to give praise and maybe offer rewards—say, taking the family out for dinner or to a play or a ball game—if the kids get good grades or do well in sports. This will make you more human and more approachable.

Interacting Socializers: They like laughing, joking, and acting silly together and want to be accepted by the family for being dynamic and fun loving. But they prefer relaxing and not having to deal with conflicts. They want to feel that their family is close-knit and can solve most of its problems by verbalizing its feelings.

The Socializer household is sometimes chaotic. That's because Socializers so often operate spontaneously, without much thought as to final outcomes. One house-hunting Socializer, for example, fell in love more with each home he saw until, finally, he realized he'd made offers and given deposits simultaneously on five different pieces of property. It took some fancy legal footwork—and considerable family debate—to get out of that one!

If you're a Socializer, you can help guard against some of your own excesses by:

• Watching your tendency to jump to conclusions. When there's a family crisis—say, a bad report card—find out all the facts before making a statement or a decision you'll regret.
• Firmly disciplining the children if the facts point to misbehavior. Avoid succumbing to your natural fear that the kids may not like you if you punish them.
• Getting into the habit of writing down significant

dates and events—and then keeping the list with you. Maybe you can keep a master schedule at work, home, and perhaps even in the car so you can stay on track!

- Organizing more efficiently the family activities (or getting someone else to do it, or help you with it).

Steady Relaters: Naturally group-oriented, Relaters enjoy sharing family feelings and reminiscences. And for them, almost everything *is* a family affair. They like to get everyone involved in making family decisions about things like vacations and major purchases. Many Relaters want home life to be a peaceful retreat where stresses seldom occur, so they often make sacrifices and act as peacemakers.

If you're a Relater, here's what you might do to improve family relations:

- Speak up when you're upset about something. Because you do that so infrequently, you'll definitely get your family's attention.
- Don't be so wedded to the status quo that the family routine becomes numbing. Show some spontaneity!
- Recognize that disagreements and unsettling events will occur. Such is life! Experience it, don't recoil from it.
- Be more decisive. Take the initiative, when appropriate, rather than always assembling a family parliament to discuss whether everyone is pleased with everything.

Cautious Thinkers: Family life is often hard, too, for Thinkers, because there's so much about it that's illogical. Thinkers want family members to be cautious, disciplined, and interested in quality. When they're not, Thinkers can seem emotionally hard to reach, even by their loved ones. They're more comfortable *thinking* about their feelings than expressing them to others. And they may even gravitate toward hobbies and interests—say, computers or novels—that are essentially solitary activities.

If you're a Thinker, you can adapt better to your family by:

- Accepting the fact that no one is right all the time—not even you.
- Taking care to voice your feedback or criticism in a caring way.
- Easing up by not taking so many events or conditions around the home so seriously.
- Talking more about your feelings, or what you think of your feelings. ("My sense is that the camping trip wasn't as much fun as usual. I know I was a bit disappointed. Did others feel that way, too?")

9. *Remember that your children have personality styles, too.* The principles of **The Platinum Rule** are universal and apply in any country or culture—and to people of any age or size. Using **The Platinum Rule** can help parents see how children often aren't trying to be devilish or ornery. Instead, they're acting, just as adults do, in ways intended to meet their personality needs. You can adapt to your child's behavior by using the same methods we've outlined for dealing with adults.

Dominant Director Kids: If yours is a Director child, he or she will probably be a handful: "headstrong," "difficult," or "demanding" are terms you've probably uttered or heard. That's because young Directors show early signs that they're self-contained and interested less in socializing than in results—running the fastest, singing the loudest, drawing the best, or otherwise proving themselves superior.

Another sure sign of a young Director is the quickness with which they shed shyness and seek out what they need. They'll quickly learn to go to a security guard, teacher, clerk, or other adult if they want help in locating something, whether it be a "missing" parent, an elusive fact, or a hard-to-find toy in the store.

But rather than just labeling a Director child, the parent needs to affirm the child's natural need for control over his or her environment. Such understanding can produce surprising benefits. Allowing the young Director to have authority over pets, toys, or his or her own room, for example, may help channel this need in a positive way.

Interacting Socializer Kids: Young Socializers may get reprimanded at school for talking. But for them, talking about any experience, good or bad, is as natural as breathing and almost as hard to curtail. Of the four types, Socializer children respond the most positively to treats and rewards if they've performed well. And, speaking of performance, anything that smacks of potential stardom—plays, recitals, pageants, sports, even cracking jokes—attracts them irresistibly because it fulfills their need for special attention.

As a parent, you can best help your Socializer children by gently reminding them that no one can realistically please everybody all the time and that popularity, while fun and desirable, is not the sole measure of worth.

Steady Relater Kids: You're probably the proud parent of a Relater if you've ever said, "That kid has never given me a moment of trouble." They say "thank you" without being prodded, take a nap when they're supposed to, and may even do their homework without being threatened.

Of course, there are trade-offs. They're not over-achievers by nature. So you may need to coax them to make friends, for instance, when you move to a new neighborhood. And you'll likely be forced to lean on them a bit to get them to try out for cheerleader or give a speech at school. To stretch, they're probably going to need a nudge from you and plenty of praise.

Cautious Thinker Kids: These children often seem more serious than their peers and more addicted to organization. Like the Relaters, they enjoy watching and observing. But Thinker kids usually keep their emotions to themselves. They often do well in school because they're naturally compliant and therefore not as likely to question openly the teacher or the rules. In fact, of all the types, these are the kids who wouldn't want to be embarrassed by not meeting commonly accepted standards, let alone failing to meet their own high expectations.

You can help your Thinker children by recognizing their sensitive nature and making a point not to crowd them. You also can spur their growth by ensuring an especially comforting environment—heavy on love and assurance, light on contention—so that they'll be encouraged to emerge further from their shell.

10. *Improve your romantic rapport.* Compatibility is the whole point of dating. At work, we may adapt to other behavioral styles to get a certain job done. But in dating, developing rapport isn't just preferable, it's the goal.

Using **The Platinum Rule** will help you understand your partner's behavior. You'll see that he or she is not just "being that way" with you, but instead is acting out of deep-seated needs. Having found that out, the rest is up to you.

Let's take a quick look at how the four styles approach dating and how you might best increase rapport with a partner of another style:

Dominant Directors: Not surprisingly, they're aggressive in courtship. (I've heard it said—only half-jokingly— that Directors favor "love at first sight" because it saves time!) They enjoy the role of pursuer and like to set the unwritten rules for the relationship. Not shy, they'll usually ask for whatever they want and in myriad ways may seek to take command of the relationship. Directors like a lot of control in deciding where to go and what to do. They speak frankly, and their requests can sometimes sound an awful lot like demands.

If you're involved with a Director, you can increase rapport by:

- Trying your hand at negotiating, too—such as, "You picked this movie. Next time I get to choose. Agreed?"
- Repeating, when necessary, that you don't agree with a decision and want your opinion heard.
- Letting them know you appreciate it when they listen patiently, and are distressed when they don't.

Interacting Socializers: Of all the styles, Socializers report falling in and out of love (or, at least, infatuation) more often than their counterparts. Because they're comfortable with newness and change, it's rather natural for them to keep their options—and their eyes—wide open. They prefer a lighthearted date who'll tell them how much they're admired. And they may look for an especially attractive, socially acceptable match who'll provide the added bonus of favorable attention.

If you're dating a Socializer, you could:

- Lessen the whirlwind by warmly explaining that quiet moments are sometimes appropriate. ("What if we stayed home tonight for a change and just played Scrabble?")
- Proceed spontaneously on some things, but insist on a plan for other activities.
- Encourage their dreams—but don't take each brainstorm at face value. In fact, you'll probably want to mentally divide their "great ideas" at least by half before seriously thinking about implementing them.

Steady Relaters: Many Relaters seem to fear rejection in the dating market, so they may not be as quick as others to follow up on their romantic instincts or to bounce back as quickly if rebuffed, even mildly. Sometimes ultraconsiderate Relaters will act like a doormat, letting the date pick the time, the restaurant, the food, the entertainment, almost everything—until their partner tires of making all the choices. Relaters like to see sincere, steady pursuit by the other person, with the Relater seeking to gauge whether he or she is not "too far out ahead."

You can aid the Relater by:

- Injecting some spontaneity into the romance— suggest going someplace on the spur of the moment.
- Showing them that the two of you can be at odds without it becoming a major conflict.
- Support them in verbalizing their thoughts and feelings. ("No . . . now please don't acquiesce on me! Tell me what you'd really like to do—go to the party, take in a play, or just go for a long walk?")

Cautious Thinkers: Dating can be hard work for Thinkers because they do so much analyzing of what's happening and the possible consequences. Usually, the naturally cerebral Thinkers prefer a date with some substance or depth, and they want sufficient freedom in a relationship to allow for some "alone" time. In addition, they like their dates to be punctual, organized, rational, and true to their word.

If you're dating a Thinker, you'll want to:

- Help them tap their sense of humor by sharing and discussing funny situations.
- Encourage them to let their guard down occasionally and do something off-the-wall. ("Sure, why not go to the Halloween party in drag? It'll be a kick!")
- Show them that you don't care about them being perfect; you just care about them.

CHAPTER 9

◆

EXPANDING YOUR VISION AND IDEAS

A kindergarten teacher asked a student what she was drawing. "I'm drawing a picture of God," the child quickly answered.

"But, sweetheart," said the teacher, "no one knows what God looks like."

"They will in a minute!" the child replied, according to a story told by Sheila Murray Bethel in her book *Making a Difference.*

Charismatic people possess a similar, almost childlike faith in their vision and their ability to create change. People will follow leaders whose vision inspires them and makes their lives more meaningful.

In fact, having a strong, infectious vision will go a long way toward compensating for a lack of some other charismatic attributes. Einstein, for example, or Eleanor Roosevelt, or Bill Gates, whom I mentioned earlier, aren't people who immediately leap to mind as being as dashing or debonair as stereotypically "charismatic" leaders.

But their strong ideas or vision may have more than made up for other shortcomings. (Have you heard the computer-industry joke? "What do you call a nerd fifteen years from now?" The answer: "Boss.") Their vision, it can be argued, transformed them into charismatic leaders. The strength of their ideas, and the passion with which they held them, gave them a different brand of personal magnetism. Warren Bennis, author of the best-selling book *Leaders*, says that being able to articulate your vision in a way that's easily understood, desirable, and energizing is the spark of leadership genius.

In this chapter, you'll learn about the famous and the not-so-famous who have had great impact because of their ideas and their fervor for them. We'll talk about the process most of these people went through to shape their vision and how you can do the same, thus maximizing your charisma.

THE CAPSTONE OF CHARISMA

In many ways, possessing vision is the capstone of the seven keys to charisma. To have the other six but to lack vision is akin to being all dressed up with no place to go. Being supremely able to communicate, adapt, and persuade as well as effectively use time and space and send out a positive image is wonderful.

But you still need something to say about something you care about. Lacking that, you may have a perfection of means and a confusion of ends. You could be like a person with an ax cutting daisies.

But having a vision, a sense of what you want and need to do, gives purpose and unity to the other aspects of your charisma. You might think of your total charisma as a locomotive. If the first six elements are the wheels, then vision is the engine. If the wheels are on track, the engine—the vision—can turn them, taking you where you want to go.

QUICK QUIZ: YOUR VISION AND IDEAS

For each pair of statements below, distribute three points between the two alternatives (A and B), depending on how characteristic of you the statement is. Although some pairs of statements may seem equally true for you, assign more points to the alternative that is more representative of your behavior most of the time.

Examples:

- If A is very characteristic of you and B is very uncharacteristic, write "3" next to A and "0" next to B.
- If A is more characteristic of you than B, write "2" next to A and "1" next to B.
- If B is very characteristic of you and A is very uncharacteristic, write "3" next to B and "0" next to A.

. . . and so on.

1A___I often think about what I'd really like to be doing.

1B___I try to keep focused on the current task, without wasting much time on daydreaming.

2A___I keep a written list of specific goals, which I update periodically.

2B___I know what I'd like to accomplish, but I don't feel I need to write it down.

3A___I have a personal mission statement.

3B___I know who I am without resorting to props.

4A___I rarely brood about failures.

4B___Failures, it's true, can often get me down, at least for a while.

5A___I'm always seeking feedback about how I'm performing.

5B___A tough self-critic, I am more honest than any outsider is likely to be. Thus, I rarely seek outside opinion about my performance.

6A___I usually make realistic goals and pursue them doggedly.

6B___I tend to get excited about new goals, then lose interest when, and if, I fall short.

7A___I think I'm pretty good at prioritizing my tasks.

7B___I sometimes get overwhelmed by the sheer number of tasks I've outlined for myself.

8A___I have thought a lot about what the most important thing in life is for me.

8B___My interests in life are so varied that it's hard to choose one objective that transcends all others.

9A___I know what my strengths are, and I strive principally to build upon those.

9B___Mainly, I work to reduce or eliminate my weaknesses.

10A___I frequently make it a point to get away from it all—no TV, no phone, no family or work obligations—and just think.

10B___My life is so filled with activity that there's little time for contemplation.

SCORING:

Please add point totals under "A" and enter here: _____

Please add point totals under "B" and enter here: _____

Now let's take a look at how you scored on this segment. If your "A" score is significantly greater than your "B" score (and if you were truly honest!), you are fairly strong in this aspect of charisma. The more lopsided your "A" score, the stronger your present potential for fostering vision. If your "A" score exceeds your "B" by, say, a 2-to-1 margin, your vision "glass" is far fuller than most.

Conversely, if your "B" score approximates your "A" score, you may have identified an improvement opportunity. And if the "B" score is higher than your "A," that's an indication that you need lots of work in this area.

WHAT DO YOU REALLY CARE ABOUT?

What do you feel passionately about? What do you care *really* deeply about? Whatever your objective—whether it's ending world hunger or ensuring better care for stray animals—you'll never influence anyone to change their ideas or take action if you don't feel strongly about it yourself.

How do you get such passionate vision? Well, the process probably varies somewhat from person to person. But for starters, a common denominator is recognizing what I call the need gap, which I briefly mentioned earlier.

That's the gap between *what is* and *what could be*. This disparity is the breeding ground for vision. This ability to see deficiencies in existing situations and act on them is one of the skills that separates the charismatic leader from, say, just a manager or an administrator. The manager can, so to speak, make the buses run on time. But the charismatic leader sees the need for whole new routes—or maybe even whole new modes of transportation.

Consider Bill W. and Dr. Bob. They started out in the 1950s in a small Midwest steel town with nothing but their own shattered lives—and an idea. They founded Alcoholics Anonymous. The simplicity of its twelve-step program, with its credo of "love and service," was a vision that has changed millions of lives.

Or take Carl Stotz, an almost penniless Williamsport, Pennsylvania, baseball fan who during the Depression liked to play ball with his two young nephews. As historian Garry Wills recounts in his book *Certain Trumpets*, Stotz wondered why the boys had to use clumsy grown-up gloves, swing a bat that was far too big for them, and do an imaginary play-by-play "broadcast."

So he acted on his vision. He found an unused lot and devised the dimensions of a kid-sized field. He asked around for other boys to play and other men to coach or maybe to umpire. He went to fifty-six companies before he found one willing to cough up the thirty dollars it took to field a youth team in 1938.

He then persuaded local sportswriters to cover the early games and recruited friends, relatives, and fellow volunteers to build bleachers, embroider team names on uniforms, and perform dozens of other tasks. He drew up rules that would let all boys play, even if it meant having four outfielders rather than an extra kid sitting on the bench.

His modest concept grew into—you've probably guessed it by now—Little League, a sports program that has affected more lives than any other. Baseball had risen from an old child's game in the nineteenth century to become the modern sport for the American masses. Stotz's vision returned it to the children.

A purist, Stotz eventually became estranged from the Little League organization as it grew into a big business and became more of a high-pressure pastime. But until his death in 1992, he could take pride that it was his vision—and energy and hard work—that had created recreation and character-building opportunities for millions of young people.

THE STEPS TO CREATING VISION

I think there are three stages to arriving at a vision that'll help make you a charismatic leader. The first is your *defining moment*. That's when, as the saying goes, "the lightbulb goes on." Something clicks in your skull. You realize you're on to something really exciting.

This can occur in the throes of a busy day at work, but often it's a solitary experience. "If we are to survive, we must have ideas, vision, and courage," historian Arthur M. Schlesinger, Jr., wrote in *The Decline of Heroes*. "These things are rarely produced by committees. Everything that matters in our intellectual and moral life begins with an individual confronting his own mind and conscience in a room by himself."

About fifteen years ago, for example, it occurred to Robert L. Johnson, a black businessman who worked for the National Cable Television Association, that someone was going to target black media consumers. "I figured," he later said, "why not me?"

An associate describes Johnson this way: "He is the kind of person who is able to create a vision or an idea of what he wants to accomplish, and once he has, he's fantastic at persuading other businesspeople to support him." Johnson's BET Holdings, Inc. (for Black Entertainment Television) aims to be to African-American consumers what the Walt Disney Company is to families in general, and already BET reaches 40 million households. Meanwhile, Johnson is transferring the BET brand to magazines, radio, film production, electronic retailing, and other interests. Aiming at becoming a one-stop shopping spot for advertisers to reach black consumers, BET employs 450 people and brings in $115 million in sales—all from Robert Johnson's idea that there was a need for black programming and his "Why not me?" approach.

Filling an Existing Need

Not every idea you have will be a breakthrough, a defining moment, though. Your idea might be initially exciting to you. But to qualify as visionary it must appeal to the values and needs of the people you're seeking to lead.

Remember, a big part of charisma is chemistry between the leader and the led. So you'll have little luck in the long term if you merely have a solution in search of a problem. The Edsel automobile. The "new" Coca-Cola. The rush to get the United States to adopt the metric system for all its measurements. These were all ideas somebody had, but they were ideas that didn't fill a widespread need.

So if you exaggerate the need gap, or try to create a phony one, you'll lose credibility. What's required is some serious study to make sure you're filling an existing need, not a manufactured one or one that appeals to you alone.

Molly Wetzel's defining moment, for example, came after much work and worry. A business consultant and single mother in Berkeley, California, she watched helplessly as her once middle-class neighborhood fell into decay. A house nearby, owned by an absentee landlord, had become a haven for prostitutes, drug dealers, and other criminals. Her teenage daughter couldn't walk down the street without getting solicited for sex, and her young son was robbed of 75 cents at gunpoint. "It was a nightmare," Wetzel said.

For eighteen months, she and her neighbors appealed to police and local politicians, but to no avail. Then one day she read an article about a California appellate court decision that declared small-claims court to be a proper place for settling disputes involving complex social issues. That was her defining moment. She knew the need, knew it very well. And now she knew the answer.

Though she had no legal background, she soon corralled eighteen neighbors—ranging in age from three to sixty-five—and together they sued the absentee property owner for destroying the neighborhood. They won. Wetzel and the neighbors were awarded $2,000 each, and within two weeks the property owner had evicted the drug dealers. Today the neighborhood is thriving—and so is Safe Streets Now!, a nonprofit organization Wetzel formed to help other neighborhoods fight crime by using small-claims courts or the threat of lawsuits.

"After we won the case, my phone never stopped ringing," Wetzel said. At last count, Safe Streets Now! had twenty-three chapters from California to Massachusetts, and their actions had resulted in the shutting down of 485 trouble spots, such as drug houses, liquor stores, and motels that were hangouts for criminals.

Wetzel's efforts have been lauded by Harvard University's Kennedy School of Government and others. But apart from the statistics and the kudos, the real triumph, Wetzel says, is what neighbors learned about themselves and each other. "New leaders emerge. When they fight crime successfully, they realize that they can improve the parks and the schools—they can do anything." And the greatest lesson of all, she says, is that children watch their parents solve problems without violence.

Though she lacked an impressive title or the backing of a large organization, Molly Wetzel believed strongly in what she was offering, could explain how it filled a need, and was willing to work hard to develop the idea.

Creating the Mission

To get anything significant accomplished, you must see the need, as well as work hard, possess energy, and demonstrate drive. But to truly influence others, you also need a *mission*. That's the second stage of fashioning a vision. It's what gives purpose, context, and stamina to your defining moment.

It isn't enough just to come up with a "mission statement" that merely sounds good or looks sharp on paper or in an annual report, though that's a start. Instead, to be effective your mission has got to come from your heart. It's got to grow out of a sense of what's important in your life and in your world. The deeper your passion for the mission, the more it will attract others, thus enhancing your charisma.

Further, an effective mission must reflect the "need gap" by being sensitive to what other people want and need. The most effective missions involve helping others. "Leaders are more likely to be viewed as charismatic if they make self-sacrifices, take personal risks, and incur high costs to achieve the vision they espouse," according to Gary Yukl, a student of charisma and author of *Leadership in Organizations*. "Trust appears to be an important component of charisma, and followers have more trust in a leader who advocates a strategy in a manner reflecting concerns for followers rather than self-interest."

Thus, Bill W. and Dr. Bob weren't just helping themselves, they were helping alcoholics everywhere redeem themselves. With Molly Wetzel, her mission was making a lot of neighborhoods more livable, not just hers.

Often it's acquiring that mission that catapults people into a leadership role, that puts them in a position to exercise personal power. Steve Jobs and Steve Wozniak didn't start up Apple Computer just to make money or to make people more efficient; their mission was to develop a "user-friendly" machine that would revolutionize people's lives. Their sense of purpose propelled them to perform brilliantly. And, characteristically, when they later sought to attract John Sculley, widely respected as a marvelous marketer, they didn't emphasize money or prestige, both of which he already had in abundance as Pepsi's president and CEO.

Instead, according to Sculley's autobiography, Jobs and Sculley were walking near Sculley's home when Jobs asked, "So, what do you want to do, John? Do you want to sell sugared water for the rest of your life—or do you want a chance to change the world?" Sculley, faced with that kind of challenge and that kind of vision, *knew* what he had to do. He acquired a new mission and joined Apple.

CARING ENOUGH

Candy Lightner's defining moment came in 1980 when her daughter Cari was killed by a drunk driver. Her anger soon turned to her mission: a burning desire to do something about such wasteful tragedies. Within a few days, she held a meeting with a few friends—and that was the beginning of Mothers Against Drunk Driving, better known as MADD.

Today, it's one of the most powerful citizen groups in the world. MADD has spawned hundreds of new laws against drunk driving in all fifty states, and off-shoots—like SADD (Students Against Drunk Driving)—have been formed to encourage citizen action further.

Candy Lightner had no position power when she began. Yet she is living proof of Andrew Jackson's famous epigram: "One man with courage makes a majority." Or, in this case, one woman. "If you care enough," Lightner says, "you can accomplish anything."

THE EVOLUTION OF A MISSION

You may have noticed a few things about the missions we've talked about so far. First, none of them—not Bill W. or Dr. Bob, Carl Stotz, Molly Wetzel, Candy Lightner, or Steve Jobs and Steve Wozniak—had as their mission to make a lot of money or get their faces on, say, the cover of *People* magazine. Some of them may have coincidentally gotten rich and famous, but that wasn't their mission, and it shouldn't be yours.

Second, probably none of them set out saying to themselves, "I'm going to be a leader with a mission." Instead, their mission kind of evolved from what they were doing at work, or at home, or in their spare time. And then it grew and inspired others.

If your mission coincides with your occupation, great! But if it doesn't, that may be okay too. As Donald Clifton and Paula Nelson wrote in their book, *Soar with Your Strengths*, "If our work gives us purpose, then we have an advantage. But many people have a mission separate from their work, and their job is the means to support it."

You may work as an engineer, for example, but spend your free time as an amateur pilot flying doctors into Third World countries. Or having an aging, infirm parent may motivate you to get involved in seniors' programs. A woman I know gave birth to a severely disabled child, and that experience led her to go back to school, become a psychologist, and specialize in helping other parents of handicapped children.

A Positive Attitude

Another common characteristic of many of the best missions, as I mentioned, is that they were created to serve others. When people or companies think only of how many units they can produce or sell, something happens to the spirit.

"Painters must want to paint above all else," concludes noted University of Chicago psychologist Mihaly Csikszentmihalyi, who's studied peak performance. "If the artist in front of the canvas begins to wonder how much he will sell it for, or what the critics will think of it, he won't be able to pursue original avenues. Creative achievements depend on single-minded immersion."

Do you recall when Detroit automakers focused on how many cars they could sell rather than how well they could serve the American people with quality transportation? They lost enormous market share.

Again, keep in mind that followers of a charismatic person must have a cause, a reason, that bonds them to that leader. And to be enticing, that cause has to be bigger than just the leader. Thus, choosing to try to make a difference in even a small way is helpful and important as well as noble.

As usual, your attitude can affect how you choose to frame your mission. Perhaps you look around and say, "Here I am, stuck in a dead-end job. How can I hope to improve my charisma? How can I possibly develop a mission?"

But where we are or what happens to us is not as important as what we think about where we are or what happens to us. Maybe you work in a low-paying job at an art gallery. Looked at from a cynical perspective, you sell expensive paintings to rich people, and that doesn't strike you as either noble or a good base for exercising charisma. But what if you thought of what you do as helping to spread beauty, or helping artists make a living, and, thus, spawning creativity? Or maybe you're an insurance agent, hardly a glamorous or altruistic role at first glance—unless you think of the families or businesses you're protecting, the financial safety net you're developing for all sorts of people.

My point is, maybe we can't all have missions echoing the grand but simple nobility espoused by Salvation Army founder William Booth: "Others." But we can all look outside ourselves as we try to figure out our life's purpose. And looking outside ourselves will not only help us fashion a mission, but it will also help draw people to us and enhance our charisma.

From the Momentous to the Mundane

Candy Lightner, Steve Jobs, and some of the others mentioned became, to some degree, national figures whose defining moments turned into missions and whose impact we can understand and perhaps applaud. But vision doesn't need to spring from tragedy or aspire to greatness. It doesn't need to snare headlines or be cosmic in its scope.

Your mission can mean that by just having faith you can accomplish something—and impart that faith to others. Take Edward Lowe. It's hard to imagine a vision more mundane than his.

In the winter of 1947, he was working in his father's sawdust business in Cassopolis, Michigan, when he received a visit from a cat-loving neighbor. Her sand-filled kitty box had frozen, and she wanted to replace the contents with sawdust. But young Lowe convinced her to try a bag of kiln-dried granulated clay he had in the trunk of his '43 Chevy coupe. It was a highly absorbent mineral that his father, who sold sawdust to factories to sop up oil and grease spills, had begun offering as a fireproof alternative.

When the cat lady came back a few days later asking for more, Lowe knew he was on to something. It was his defining moment. He produced ten five-pound sacks, called the new product Kitty Litter, and offered them at 65 cents apiece. People laughed because sand, which had always been used for cat boxes, was selling for only a penny a pound.

Undeterred, Lowe gave away the ten sacks. When those ten customers returned, asking for Kitty Litter by name, it was Lowe's turn to laugh. A business, a brand, and a mission had just been born.

Adapting clay for use as a cat-box filler made felines more acceptable as household pets and made Lowe wealthy. Several years before his death in 1995, Lowe sold his Kitty Litter operations for more than $200 million. Meanwhile, cats had surpassed dogs as the most popular American pet, in no small part due to improved hygiene brought about by Lowe's innovation.

The Third Step

Having a breakthrough thought (a defining moment) and an overarching philosophy (a mission) will only get you so far. You've got to transform those thoughts and that philosophy into action. You do that by setting and accomplishing goals.

You must not only believe you have a better sales plan, a better way to run the school board, a better solution for reducing health-care costs, an environmentally friendly mousetrap—or whatever you have. You've also got to figure out how you're going to accomplish your mission.

So to be charismatic and to bring your vision to reality, you need to present a strategy that seems reasonable and attractive. That's the third step in creating and giving life to a vision.

A goal differs from a mission. The latter is long term; usually, in fact, lifelong. But a goal is more timebound, existing only to be achieved. A politician, for example, might have experienced terrible poverty or discrimination as a youth (his defining moment). His mission became to enact laws that would right economic wrongs or free a whole class of people.

But his goal would be, first, to get elected. Subsequent goals might be to get appointed to a crucial committee, introduce a strong piece of legislation, corral the needed votes, and so on. The mission stays the same, but the goals keep changing, as they must.

A Peak Performer Pushes

The temptation is to set goals too low. Most people choose not to have high standards. But only by aspiring to be the best will you achieve high levels of success.

246

A salesperson may not want to make a call on a potential new customer for fear he'll be rejected. An athlete may not want to raise the bar for fear of failure. But the peak performer guards against this mind-set.

Nadia Comaneci, the first Olympic gymnast to score a perfect "10," said, "I always underestimated what I did by saying, 'I can do better.' To be an Olympic champion you have to be a little abnormal and work harder than everyone else. Being normal is not great because you will have a boring life. I live by a code I created: Don't pray for an easy life, pray to be a strong person."

Real champions know that failing with an excuse is simply not as good as succeeding. "Only the best practice when they don't feel like it or when it is in-convenient," says Peter Vidmar, another Gold Medal–winning gymnast. "I made a clear list of objectives that I had to accomplish every day in the gym. If my workout lasted three hours, great! If the workout lasted six hours, tough luck! I wouldn't leave without accomplishing my objectives. My daily goal was to leave knowing that I had done everything I could."

SMART GOALS

Striving for and attaining goals makes life meaningful. Goals create drive and positively affect your charisma—but *only* if you set yourself to achieving them in the proper way. I've found that the letters in the word SMART are very useful in articulating goals.

SMART reminds me that my goals must be **S**pecific, **M**easurable, **A**ttainable, **R**ealistic, and **T**rackable.

Specific and *Measurable* relate to how you phrase your goal. Vagueness goes hand in hand with lack of genuine commitment. You don't think a world-class pole vaulter, for instance, just says "I want to jump higher next year." No, he has a certain height in mind.

So instead of "I will be more fit in six months so I can hike into mountains and help with a reforestation project," you might say, "In six months my resting blood pressure will be ten points lower." Or, "In six months I'll be twenty pounds lighter." "I'll be running three miles in four to six months" is more effective than "I'll be running more in four to six months."

Or if your goal is to become a standout salesperson so you eventually can rise in the firm and change its focus, you'd be better off proclaiming, "I will increase my sales next year by twenty percent" rather than "I will sell more next year."

Attainable and *Realistic* have to do with the goal, which should be just beyond your reach, making you stretch. It should be attainable, yet challenging.

If it's almost impossible to achieve, a goal can be *de*motivating. On the other hand, a goal with 100 percent chance of achievement is not really a goal; it's a given. And that defeats the purpose of goals, which is to move you forward by making you work harder, or by gathering more resources than you have in the past.

And the "T" of SMART goal-setting is *Trackable*. How will you know if you're making progress? You need to set up interim goals or checkpoints along the way. Depending on what your goal is, you might be checking your progress every day, once a week, or once every two months.

You may discover that your goal is not attainable or realistic within the time frame you've set. But be flexible about your game plan before you reconsider your goal. Nothing ever goes exactly according to plan, so you may have to make adjustments in order to stay on track and keep up your motivation.

Some other suggestions about goals:

- *Write them down.* It's one thing to think about your goals, but it's quite another to dignify them by putting them on paper. *Trust me on this!* Writing them down makes them more tangible, more meaningful, more imperative. Instead of being maybe nothing more than a vague musing, your list of goals becomes a call to arms, a goad to action, a pact with yourself.
- *Make them personal.* They must be sincere and something you *want* to do rather than something you think you *should* do. Whatever your objective, the reasons must be strong enough to fuel your desire to work to attain your goal.
- *Make them positive.* The mind can't refuse to think of something when instructed to do so. So if you say, "I will not smoke today," your mind automatically ends up thinking more about smoking than if you had said, "I will breathe only clean air today." Same purpose, more effective.

MAKING BIG TASKS SMALLER

Another trick for reaching your goals is knowing how to break large tasks into smaller ones. Or, as is sometimes said, you can eat an elephant, but only by taking one bite at a time.

I use the word *chunking* to describe this process. For instance, when I landed a contract to write my first book, *Non-Manipulative Selling*, I had six months to write it. On my "To Do" list every day of those six months was: *Write book.*

Six months went by, no book. The publisher gave me another three months. For three more months *Write book* appeared daily on my "To Do" list. Still no book. Finally, the publisher gave me a final three months, or else I'd lose the contract.

Fortunately, Karl Albrecht, author of *Service America*, gave me the concept of "chunking." He asked me how many pages I had to write. Answer: 180. How many days to write it? Answer: 90. So he told me that every day my "To Do" list should contain this note: *Write 2 pages of book.* I *must* write two pages. If I got on a roll, I could write four or five. But the next day, I still had to write a minimum of two. By following his advice, *I finished the book in thirty days!*

A final technique for managing your goals comes from Dr. John Lee, author, speaker, and time-management expert. He says when a new task pops up, or an old one resurfaces, apply one of the four D's: **D**rop it, **D**elegate it, **D**elay it, or **D**o it. Consciously choosing one of those strategies every time you face a task will keep things progressing smoothly.

THERE'S HOPE

While all seven elements of charisma are important, it's clear to me that vision is even more so. If you're not a gifted communicator like, say, Winston Churchill, or don't possess the panache of a John F. Kennedy or a Margaret Thatcher, you still can influence others positively in ways big or small.

In his excellent study *Leading Minds*, Harvard educator Howard Gardner points out that our most famous leaders usually are "direct"—generalists who confront their public face to face. But others are "indirect" leaders who exert enormous impact through their ideas and the works they create. Creative artists, scientists, and experts in various disciplines lead indirectly, through their work, while those who command institutions and nations lead directly in the more traditional way: public appearances, speeches, legislation, and the like.

In both cases, leaders relate "stories"—their ideas, their visions—that help establish their identity. Gardner contrasts, for example, Einstein, "a solitary thinker armed with only a succinct physics equation," with the powerful triumvirate of Stalin, Churchill, and Roosevelt that met in Tehran in 1943 to plan a conclusion to World War II. "Who ultimately had the greater influence?" he asks. The three strong world leaders changed, for a time, the world political map. But the lonely physicist, who preferred "the laboratory of his imagination," may have changed mankind forever.

Charles Darwin led no organization, nor did Margaret Mead. Neither was a strong leader in the conventional sense. But their messages—their "visions," if you will—had, and continue to have, a huge effect on how we view the world.

So, again, there's room for individuality in how you lead, how you employ your charisma. Most of us won't found schools of thought, lead major organizations, or otherwise emblazon our way into the history books. But you and I can use our charismatic skills, present and future, to be the best people we can be and to influence others positively. The surest way to do that is, first, to hone your vision.

A MISSION THAT MATTERS

Sheila Murray Bethel, whom I mentioned before, says there are three major roadblocks to building what she calls "a mission that matters": first, thinking that you're too old or too young or too *anything* to have a mission; second, putting off getting started; and, third, doing nothing because you feel you can do so little.

So there! That's the challenge: *Get started on creating your vision, whatever it might be.* As Helen Keller, sightless but inspirational to so many, once said, "I long to accomplish a great and noble task, but it is my chief duty to accomplish small tasks as if they were great and noble."

JUMP-STARTING YOUR SENSE OF VISION

1. *Listen to your yearnings.* Don't dismiss your daydreams, or for that matter, your nocturnal dreams, either. They may be signals from your mind and body of some unconscious attraction. And don't listen just to those that fall under the heading of "money" or "things." Think about nonmonetary, nonmaterial rewards such as a job you'd love or more quality time with your family or doing something to help mankind. What's important is what's important to you *personally*.

Sometimes it's helpful to recall your childhood or youth. What propelled your dreams back then? Where did your imagination take you? What most influenced you?

Chuck Williams, for instance, got his first taste of fine cooking at age seven from his grandmother, who owned a restaurant. He didn't go to college, but instead worked as a mechanic, then a contractor in Sonoma, California, where he also was involved with a local cooking group. Then he became fascinated with the kitchen equipment he saw while on a trip to France.

Two years later, he bought a hardware shop to which he later added housewares and cookware. The store was an instant success and the seed of what would become the Williams-Sonoma retailing empire of upscale kitchen stores, cookbooks, accessories, and catalog sales. Williams, who readily admitted to having few management skills, made up for that in creativity and instinct—and in following up on his fond childhood memories and interest in cooking.

And it's not just the fun or fanciful moments you should recall. If you were poor, maybe helping others escape poverty could be your mission as an adult. If you were abused, maybe abuse prevention is an area where, in your heart of hearts, you would like to make a difference.

2. *Seek feedback.* "Unfortunately," said Dr. Norman Vincent Peale, "most people would rather be ruined by praise than saved by criticism." But getting others to give you honest, constructive feedback may help put your mission and your goals in perspective. They may uncover a diamond you thought was just a pebble, thus sending you off in a better direction.

You should be able to get a source of feedback for free from friends and colleagues. But if you can't, hire it. It soon will pay for itself.

3. *Focus on your strengths.* You may have heard the adage "Don't try to teach a pig to sing—it wastes your time and annoys the pig." Too often we try to force ourselves to become detail people when we're not, or to climb the management ranks when what we enjoy and excel at is the rank-and-file work.

Ask yourself: What am I really good at? What do I most enjoy? And think about a mission and goals related to those answers.

253

4. *Identify and manage your weaknesses.* While concentrating on your strengths, do all you can to keep your weaknesses from dragging you down, either in terms of performance or just in the sense of taking up a lot of your time with fretting.

If you're great at sales but terrible at filling out reports, for example, maybe you ought to hire a part-time administrative assistant or swap duties with another employee so you'll have the time to sell and formulate your ideas about better ways to sell.

5. *Ask yourself: "What's in it for me?"* As you select your dream or goal, keep asking yourself, "Why do I want this?" and "What's in it for me?" That sounds selfish, but it's a way to keep on track and make sure you're not superimposing someone else's goals on your own. *Should* or *ought* need to take a backseat to what feels right and comfortable for you.

So look for the personally compelling reason. "My father always wanted me to follow in his footsteps" or "My boss thinks this is a good plan for me" are not good answers because a mission is not a duty or a task; it's a dream. And if the dream doesn't excite *you*, then it's probably not a good match.

6. *Write a mission statement.* Answer the question, in writing: What is it that I would really, really like to do that would utilize my strengths and make a difference? Don't worry at first about the logic or how this mission might be accomplished. It's not a plan. It's an expression of values.

Once you've got it, you may want to modify it over the years as your priorities and beliefs change. But, in any event, get the mission down on paper. Then you can figure out how best to achieve it.

7. *Take time to get away.* It's important to carve out some time to let your mind wander. Get off by yourself now and then, without the phone, fax, beeper, or TV. Unleash your imagination and see where it roams. Listen to what your heart tells you.

8. *Deal with distractions.* On the route to achieving your dream, you'll find change, risk, surprise, stress, and perhaps even failure. But if you're committed, you'll adapt.

"Gee," you might say to yourself, "I've never run a marathon in a hailstorm before. It'll probably slow me down, but it'll slow the others down, too. Meanwhile, it'll give me experience running in unusual conditions, and it won't necessarily divert me from my goal of completing a marathon."

9. *Stay in the here and now.* One of life's hardest lessons is that you can only affect the future by staying in the present. If you let your mind wander into the past and what might have been, or into the future and what problems could await you there, you'll likely lose your way.

Avoiding these extremes is what athletes call "the zone." They're not obsessing about last week's defeat or thinking ahead to how powerful next week's team is. Instead, they're fully engrossed in the process of doing the best they can, *right now*.

10. *Do it!* "The best way to predict your future," says management guru Peter F. Drucker, "is to create it." Once you know your mission and goals, that's the time to get down to doing it.

It's so in every field of endeavor. Writers must sit down and write; salespeople must sell; managers must manage; and painters must paint. Too often, though, people are locked into habits that prevent them from moving ahead. They relive yesterdays, they invent excuses, they procrastinate, they doodle in the margins of life's tablet instead of seeking to write their signature boldly. So don't give up on your dreams but, instead, pursue them with passion.

PART III

◆

PUTTING YOUR NEWFOUND CHARISMA TO WORK

CHAPTER 10

♦

A LAST NUDGE TOWARD BEING THE BEST YOU CAN BE

I've always heard it said that there are three kinds of people: those who make things happen, those who have things happen to them, and those who wonder "What happened?" The purpose of this book has been to help you propel yourself into that first category.

You *can* increase your charisma and, in large measure, take control of your destiny. As I've sought to show, you already have everything you need. Now it's up to you to take those ingredients and build the best you possible.

The fact that you've gotten this far suggests you're already motivated. But the task now is to follow through and not let your zest for self-improvement fade with the closing of the book. Success does not come to those who wait—and it doesn't wait for anyone to come to it.

I've given you a lot of improvement ideas, and it's true that some of them are difficult to carry out, requiring changing years of habit. Just reading about the possibilities, though, won't make them come true.

259

That's like leaving the porch light on for Jimmy Hoffa—a well-meaning exercise in false hope. So my next, and final, step is to nudge you toward a vigorous, consistent follow-up.

I've already recommended ways to improve your silent message, or image; how to speak well; how to listen more intently; how to be a better persuader or motivator; how to use space and time to your best advantage; how to adapt to different personalities; and how to expand your vision and ideas. And, at the end of each of those chapters, you've been offered an additional ten ways to jump-start your use of that particular skill.

In this final section, I am going to toss out a few more suggestions to underscore those ideas. I'll try to do so a bit lightheartedly, so you don't feel I'm nagging you, but rather, I hope, grabbing your attention and launching you toward new levels of personality power.

SUGGESTION NO. 1:
YOU ARE WHO YOU THINK YOU ARE

Speaking of people with personality power, you need to realize that you *are* one. Hold that positive image. What you see is what you become. So make "charismatic" a mandatory part of your private self-description and visualize yourself exuding personal magnetism. This is important because *you're* the first person you need to convince. Do that—and you're on your way!

I'm reminded of a story Katharine Hepburn told about breaking into Hollywood in the thirties. She was a tall, coltish New England actress of aristocratic bearing at a time when the norm for female movie stars tended toward the small, sweet, and cuddly.

But she was confident and had such a good self-image that, she recalled, she thrust herself on the movie colony "as though I were a basket of flowers." What a wonderful image! Her sense of self was so strong that she could imagine offering herself up as a sort of gift of beauty and grace. And, of course, it worked!

Again, having a winning self-image precedes success; it doesn't follow it. And the Hepburn story again shows that.

SUGGESTION NO. 2:
YOUR INFLUENCE HAS NEVER MATTERED MORE

It's easy to fall prey to cynical, or pessimistic, thoughts and axioms, such as "Them that has, gets," or "Leaders are born, not made." But the truth is, that's nonsense.

If those with so-called natural ability to influence others don't cultivate the right skills, they'll fall short of their potential. Give me a person without the supposed "natural" talent and let me train him or her in the skills in this book, and I'll put my money on that person every time.

What's more, as I mentioned, such skills have never been more in demand. If you can develop your charisma, you'll likely be a hot property. As recently as a decade or two ago, that wasn't necessarily true. Then, in business and elsewhere, we had strict hierarchies where everyone knew his or her role and automatically followed the boss's lead.

Surprise! That's no longer true. The command-and-control structure largely went out with dial phones and leisure suits. Whether you're talking about businesses, churches, community groups, civic associations, or athletic teams, autocracy is waning. Personal power is eclipsing position power—and the key to personal power is not issuing edicts but galvanizing people, inspiring them, persuading them.

So, all in all, we're lucky to be living now when life is more fluid and we can more readily make our influence felt.

SUGGESTION NO. 3:
APATHY IS A MAJOR SOCIAL PROBLEM—
BUT WHO CARES?

Actually, it *is*—and we all should care because it's enthusiasm, not apathy, that makes the world go 'round. John Wesley, the famous founder of Methodism, was asked how he was able to attract such crowds when he preached. He replied, "I just set myself on fire and people will come from miles to watch me burn."

Setting yourself on fire with enthusiasm will fuel your charisma. But enthusiasm doesn't necessarily mean you must be an extrovert. The Directors and Socializers mentioned in Chapter 8 are naturally enthusiastic people, and, of course, they're extroverts. But that doesn't mean you Relaters and Thinkers have been handed a life sentence of apathy. It just means you'll go about the business of being enthusiastic from a different angle.

Being enthusiastic isn't merely talking energetically and gesturing wildly about your passion. It can take a quieter path. Maybe your enthusiasm is revealed by the earnestness and persistence with which you seek to get others involved. Maybe it's shown by your strength of commitment, your refusal to become discouraged. Maybe it's that spark in your eye, or that warm smile, and the unmistakable genuineness that emanates from you as you explain, again and again, your mission.

SUGGESTION NO. 4:
WHEREVER YOU ARE, THERE YOU ARE

Most of us will not lead revolutions, turn around ailing corporations, or start new social movements. But the basic tools of charisma are available—and useful—in small arenas as well as large.

In short, don't think you can only use the skills I've mentioned if you're a big shot, like a manager, a department head, or a member of the board of directors. Whether you're a peon or a potentate, you have the potential to be influential. Maybe it's only at the board meeting of the local Little League, or at the PTA. But by radiating a powerful silent message, speaking and listening well, being an effective persuader, using space and time to your advantage, adapting to other personality styles, and expanding your vision and ideas, you'll be well served, whatever the venue.

A person who could never be a Lee Iacocca on the

national stage could enjoy something like his success, say, at the Neighborhood Watch level. Or on the school board level. Or in running the family shoe-repair business.

Look for available opportunities, regardless of magnitude. That's what Art Fry did. He was just a 3M scientist singing in his church choir some twenty years ago and having trouble marking his place in the hymnal, Little pieces of paper would fall out, but bending the pages or marking them with paper clips or other devices was too permanent or damaging.

What he needed was something that would be easy to see, would stay put, but be readily removable when no longer needed. He dreamed up an idea on his own time, and then convinced his firm's higher-ups of the commercial possibilities. The result: Fry didn't have any more trouble keeping his place in the hymnal, and the world got Post-it notes, now a ubiquitous office tool and practically a household word.

SUGGESTION NO. 5:
GOOD ENOUGH, ISN'T

Mark McCormack, an attorney who represents many successful pro athletes and whom *Sports Illustrated* once called "the most powerful man in sports," says that all his star performers share an endless quest to improve. "They use any success, any victory, as a spur to greater ambition," McCormack wrote in *What They Don't Teach You at Harvard Business School.* "<u>Any goal</u>

that is attained immediately becomes the next step toward a greater, more 'unreachable' one."

So perhaps you scored pretty well on some phases of the tests in the various chapters, or you believe you're already pretty good at, say, persuading. Or maybe you've already put a few of this book's principles to work and have enjoyed some success. Terrific!

But I've failed if you translate that talent or success into self-satisfaction and complacency. Feeling you're already good enough in any area of charisma will almost certainly ensure that you aren't. The winner's real edge lies in the mind, a mind that's committed to perpetual self-improvement.

SUGGESTION NO. 6:
FAILURE IS THE LINE OF LEAST PERSISTENCE

There likely will be setbacks and occasional self-doubts on the road to maximizing your charisma. You're going to need patience and persistence. But it's important to keep moving toward your goal.

I'm reminded of a friend who had a life-changing experience in a cross-country ski race in Minnesota. He had moved there not long before. In an enthusiastic, if not realistic, effort to adapt to the local culture, he bought some skis, practiced a bit, and entered an advanced competition. He took off like a flash at the sound of the starter's gun. But after the first quarter-mile in near-zero temperatures, he knew he was in over his head, hopelessly outclassed by other competitors swiftly gliding past him. He was soon alone in a frozen wilderness, and his thoughts turned gloomily to fatigue and defeat.

He had initially hoped to finish in a couple of hours. But as the cold seared his lungs and the exertion weakened his arms and legs, he all but gave up on his goal. If there had been a way to surrender, he would have. But being in deep snow in the middle of the woods, his only way out was to ski out. So he pushed aside the pain and pessimism, and kept skiing.

He imagined a lodge with a roaring fire that might be just around the bend—but wasn't. He imagined a rescue vehicle slicing through the drifts to pick him up—which didn't. He even imagined a helicopter dropping down to whisk him away—but, of course, that never materialized.

So on and on he skied until, at last, he came to a sign: FINISH LINE, $\frac{1}{4}$ MILE. He couldn't believe it! Energized, he sprinted that last quarter mile and finished in a time not far from his original goal.

My friend often repeats that story, the winds more frigid and his muscles more aching with each retelling. It's become a part of his self-identity, and the memory of his endurance and ultimate triumph has gotten him through other of life's difficult scrapes and struggles. The moral, as he sees it, is that if you keep slogging ahead, refuse to give up, and stay as positive as you possibly can, you'll accomplish your goal, or something very close to it.

I could hardly argue with that. So even if you have trouble imagining success, keep moving along that snowy path in the woods. And before you know it, you'll have success beyond your imaginings.

SUGGESTION NO. 7:
EVEN THE BEST EXCUSE DOESN'T FEEL
AS GOOD AS SUCCESS

The world, according to author, salesman, and speaker extraordinaire Don Hutson, consists of winners and whiners. "Have you noticed that you seldom hear highly successful whining?" he asks. Instead, everyone silently cheers when whiners leave the room and take with them their own personal dark clouds that have been hovering over their heads.

Whiners make excuses; winners just get the job done. In weight-reduction classes, participants are often reminded that being thin feels better than, say, chocolate tastes. That's true for accomplishment, too. Having a good excuse for a poor performance doesn't compare with the thrill of having produced excellent results.

SUGGESTION NO. 8:
HAPPINESS IS A WAY OF TRAVELING,
NOT A DESTINATION

The only advantage of being a pessimist is that all your surprises are pleasant. But that's pretty small change compared to the big payoff that comes from projecting positive expectations.

Much of our happiness or unhappiness is caused, of course, not by what happens, but how we look at what happens. In other words, by our thinking habits. And habits can be changed.

George Walther, in his book *Power Talking*, shows how you can foster the mind-set that interprets setbacks as positive opportunities. He believes this is a skill that you can develop—one word, one phrase, one sentence at a time.

For starters, purge the words "I failed . . ." from your vocabulary, Walther urges. Replace them with "I learned . . ." to help your mind focus on the lessons involved.

Similarly, you might want to get in the habit of using "challenge" when others would say "problem," "I'll be glad to" instead of "I'll have to," and "I'm getting better at . . ." rather than "I'm no good at . . ."

The subliminal effect of changing even a few words, Walther says, can prompt your mind to come up with creative solutions rather than dreading or fleeing the problem.

SUGGESTION NO. 9:
WRITE YOUR OBITUARY

Seriously. Actually sitting down and writing it can be a marvelous exercise in goal-setting. Make it long and detailed. (After all, you *were* a person with extraordinary charisma!)

Your obituary can become your script, telling who you were, what you did, how well you were liked. If you're like most people, you'll first list your accomplishments, successes, and positions in organizations.

Then you'll revise your obit, realizing that what you want to be most remembered for is not how many initials you had after your name or how many employees were beneath you on the organization chart.

Rather, you'll probably want your life story to be about your character: What useful things did you do? How good a friend were you? What kind of a partner? How well did you behave in crises?

Write it. But understand that the only real way to have the sort of obituary you want is to start living the way you'd like to be remembered.

SUGGESTION NO. 10:
THE BEST THINGS IN LIFE AREN'T THINGS

It's been said that success is getting what you want, but happiness is wanting what you get. Or to put it another way: perspective, next to money, is the easiest thing to lose.

So, by all means, seek to increase your charisma. Try to become the most effective person you can be. Work at making a good first impression and projecting a positive image—but also try to retain self-awareness.

Look around you; *think* how you appear to others; *be alert* to the impression you're creating, or trying to create. If you try too hard to impress, or make a big to-do of the grand gesture, or come on too strong or too insensitively, you'll often end up creating a negative impression.

The best impression and the surest way to charisma often just means putting others first. It's been reported that one New York cab driver, for example, makes $30,000 more a year in tips alone than other cabbies. Why? Because he offers passengers a choice of several newspapers, cold drinks, or fresh fruit. He asks them what kind of music they'd prefer, and otherwise does his best to make his customers comfortable. In hectic, brusque Manhattan, his small acts of decency make him stand out.

Thus, folks with the most effective images often are those who are the least obtrusive about it. In fact, sometimes it's a simple act or gesture of courtesy—like announcing your first and last name when you see someone who may possibly have forgotten them—that burnishes your image, that really sets you pleasantly apart. Or maybe it's a short note of thanks for some favor. Or saying something nice and genuine about someone in front of his or her boss.

If never made, these gestures probably wouldn't be missed; that's why they're so obvious when you make them. In other words, being a genuinely good person, who cares about others and who does things because they are the right things to do, may be the ultimate key to increasing your personal magnetism, or charisma.

Always do right because, as Mark Twain said, that will gratify some people and astonish the rest.

If you'd like more information about other products and services offered by Alessandra & Associates, contact:

Alessandra & Associates
PO Box 2767
La Jolla, CA 92038-2767
Phone: 800-222-4383
Fax: 619-459-0435

To:

_____

From:

_____

Poems
for
Nighttime

Poems
for
Nighttime

STERLING
New York

STERLING
New York

An Imprint of Sterling Publishing Co., Inc.

STERLING and the distinctive Sterling logo are registered trademarks
of Sterling Publishing Co., Inc.

Cover illustration and compilation © 2022 Sterling Publishing Co., Inc.

ISBN 978-1-4549-4478-2

Library of Congress Control Number: 2021951604

Distributed in Canada by Sterling Publishing Co., Inc.
c/o Canadian Manda Group, 664 Annette Street
Toronto, Ontario M6S 2C8, Canada
Distributed in the United Kingdom by GMC Distribution Services
Castle Place, 166 High Street, Lewes, East Sussex BN7 1XU, England
Distributed in Australia by NewSouth Books
University of New South Wales, Sydney, NSW 2052, Australia

For information about custom editions, special sales, and premium and
corporate purchases, please contact Sterling Special Sales at
specialsales@sterlingpublishing.com.

Manufactured in the United States

2 4 6 8 10 9 7 5 3

sterlingpublishing.com

Interior design by Rich Hazelton

Contents

Evening

Night

Darkest Night

Evening

Song at Sunset

Walt Whitman

Splendor of ended day floating and filling me,
Hour prophetic, hour resuming the past,
Inflating my throat, you divine average,
You earth and life till the last ray gleams I sing.

Open mouth of my soul uttering gladness,
Eyes of my soul seeing perfection,
Natural life of me faithfully praising things,
Corroborating forever the triumph of things.

Illustrious every one!
Illustrious what we name space, sphere of unnumber'd
    spirits,
Illustrious the mystery of motion in all beings, even
    the tiniest insect,
Illustrious the attribute of speech, the senses, the
    body,
Illustrious the passing light—illustrious the pale
    reflection on the new moon in the western sky,
Illustrious whatever I see or hear or touch, to the last.

Good in all,
In the satisfaction and aplomb of animals,
In the annual return of the seasons,
In the hilarity of youth,
In the strength and flush of manhood,

In the grandeur and exquisiteness of old age,
In the superb vistas of death.

Wonderful to depart!
Wonderful to be here!
The heart, to jet the all-alike and innocent blood!
To breathe the air, how delicious!
To speak—to walk—to seize something by the hand!
To prepare for sleep, for bed, to look on my
  rose-color'd flesh!
To be conscious of my body, so satisfied, so large!
To be this incredible God I am!
To have gone forth among other Gods, these men
  and women I love.

Wonderful how I celebrate you and myself!
How my thoughts play subtly at the spectacles around!
How the clouds pass silently overhead!
How the earth darts on and on! and how the sun,
  moon, stars, dart on and on!
How the water sports and sings! (surely it is alive!)
How the trees rise and stand up, with strong trunks,
  with branches and leaves!
(Surely there is something more in each of the trees,
  some living soul.)

O amazement of things—even the least particle!
O spirituality of things!
O strain musical flowing through ages and continents,
  now reaching me and America!
I take your strong chords, intersperse them, and
  cheerfully pass them forward.

I too carol the sun, usher'd or at noon, or as now,
  setting,
I too throb to the brain and beauty of the earth and of
  all the growths of the earth,
I too have felt the resistless call of myself.

As I steam'd down the Mississippi,
As I wander'd over the prairies,
As I have lived, as I have look'd through my windows
  my eyes,
As I went forth in the morning, as I beheld the light
  breaking in the east,
As I bathed on the beach of the Eastern Sea, and again
  on the beach of the Western Sea,
As I roam'd the streets of inland Chicago, whatever
  streets I have roam'd,
Or cities or silent woods, or even amid the sights of
  war,
Wherever I have been I have charged myself with
  contentment and triumph.

I sing to the last the equalities modern or old,
I sing the endless finalès of things,
I say Nature continues, glory continues,
I praise with electric voice,
For I do not see one imperfection in the universe,
And I do not see one cause or result lamentable at last
  in the universe.

O setting sun! though the time has come,
I still warble under you, if none else does, unmitigated
  adoration.

To the Evening Star

William Blake

Thou fair-haired Angel of the Evening,
Now, whilst the sun rests on the mountains, light
Thy bright torch of love—thy radiant crown
Put on, and smile upon our evening bed!
Smile on our loves; and while thou drawest the
Blue curtains of the sky, scatter thy silver dew
On every flower that shuts its sweet eyes
In timely sleep. Let thy west wing sleep on
The lake; speak silence with thy glimmering eyes,
And wash the dusk with silver.—Soon, full soon,
Dost thou withdraw; then the wolf rages wide,
And the lion glares through the dun forest.
The fleeces of our flocks are covered with
Thy sacred dew: protect them with thine influence!

Evening Solace

Charlotte Brontë

The human heart has hidden treasures,
    In secret kept, in silence sealed;—
The thoughts, the hopes, the dreams, the pleasures,
    Whose charms were broken if revealed.
And days may pass in gay confusion,
    And nights in rosy riot fly,
While, lost in Fame's or Wealth's illusion,
    The memory of the Past may die.

But, there are hours of lonely musing,
    Such as in evening silence come,
When, soft as birds their pinions closing,
    The heart's best feelings gather home.
Then in our souls there seems to languish
    A tender grief that is not woe;
And thoughts that once wrung groans of anguish,
    Now cause but some mild tears to flow.

And feelings, once as strong as passions,
    Float softly back—a faded dream;
Our own sharp griefs and wild sensations,
    The tale of others' sufferings seem.
Oh! when the heart is freshly bleeding,
    How longs it for that time to be,
When, through the mist of years receding,
    Its woes but live in reverie!

And it can dwell on moonlight glimmer,
　　On evening shade and loneliness;
And, while the sky grows dim and dimmer,
　　Feel no untold and strange distress—
Only a deeper impulse given
　　By lonely hour and darkened room,
To solemn thoughts that soar to heaven,
　　Seeking a life and world to come.

It Is a Beauteous Evening

William Wordsworth

It is a beauteous evening, calm and free,
The holy time is quiet as a Nun
Breathless with adoration; the broad sun
Is sinking down in its tranquility;
The gentleness of heaven broods o'er the Sea:
Listen! the mighty Being is awake,
And doth with his eternal motion make
A sound like thunder—everlastingly.
Dear Child! dear Girl! that walkest with me here,
If thou appear untouched by solemn thought,
Thy nature is not therefore less divine:
Thou liest in Abraham's bosom all the year,
And worship'st at the Temple's inner shrine,
God being with thee when we know it not.

Between the Dusk of a Summer Night

William Ernest Henley

Between the dusk of a summer night
    And the dawn of a summer day,
We caught at a mood as it passed in flight,
    And we bade it stoop and stay.
And what with the dawn of night began
    With the dusk of day was done;
For that is the way of woman and man,
    When a hazard has made them one.

Arc upon arc, from shade to shine,
    The World went thundering free;
And what was his errand but hers and mine—
    The lords of him, I and she?
O, it's die we must, but it's live we can,
    And the marvel of earth and sun
Is all for the joy of woman and man
    And the longing that makes them one.

Dusk

James Whitcomb Riley

The frightened herds of clouds across the sky
  Trample the sunshine down, and chase the day
  Into the dusky forest-lands of gray
And sombre twilight. Far and faint, and high,
The wild goose trails his harrow, with a cry
  Sad as the wail of some poor castaway
  Who sees a vessel drifting far astray
Of his last hope, and lays him down to die.
The children, riotous from school, grow bold
  And quarrel with the wind whose angry gust
Plucks off the summer-hat, and flaps the fold
  Of many a crimson cloak, and twirls the dust
In spiral shapes grotesque, and dims the gold
  Of gleaming tresses with the blur of rust.

Sunset

Paul Laurence Dunbar

The river sleeps beneath the sky,
    And clasps the shadows to its breast;
The crescent moon shines dim on high;
    And in the lately radiant west
        The gold is fading into gray.
        Now stills the lark his festive lay,
        And mourns with me the dying day.

While in the south the first faint star
    Lifts to the night its silver face,
And twinkles to the moon afar
    Across the heaven's graying space,
        Low murmurs reach me from the town,
        As Day puts on her sombre crown,
        And shakes her mantle darkly down.

Bring me the sunset in a cup

Emily Dickinson

Bring me the sunset in a cup,
Reckon the morning's flagons up
    And say how many dew;
Tell me how far the morning leaps—
Tell me what time the weaver sleeps
    Who spun the breadth of blue!

Write me how many notes there be
In the new robin's ecstasy
    Among astonished boughs;
How many trips the tortoise makes,
How many cups the bee partakes,—
    The debauchee of dews!

Also, who laid the rainbow's piers,
Also, who leads the docile spheres
    By withes of supple blue?
Whose fingers string the stalactite,
Who counts the wampum of the night,
    To see that none is due?

Who built this little Alban House
And shut the windows down so close
    My spirit cannot see?

Who'll let me out some gala day
With implements to fly away,
    Passing pomposity?

The Evening Wind

William Cullen Bryant

Spirit that breathest through my lattice, thou
    That cool'st the twilight of the sultry day,
Gratefully flows thy freshness round my brow:
    Thou hast been out upon the deep at play,
Riding all day the wild blue waves till now,
      Roughening their crests, and scattering high
        their spray
And swelling the white sail. I welcome thee
To the scorched land, thou wanderer of the sea!

Nor I alone—a thousand blossoms round
    Inhale thee in the fulness of delight;
And languid forms rise up, and pulses bound
    Livelier, at coming of the wind of night;
And, languishing to hear thy grateful sound,
    Lies the vast inland stretched beyond the sight.
Go forth into the gathering shade; go forth,
God's blessing breathed upon the fainting earth!

Go, rock the little wood-bird in his nest,
    Curl the still waters, bright with stars, and
        rouse
The wide old wood from his majestic rest,
    Summoning from the innumerable boughs
The strange, deep harmonies that haunt his breast:
    Pleasant shall be thy way where meekly bows.

The shutting flower, and darkling waters pass,
And where the o'ershadowing branches sweep the
      grass.

The faint old man shall lean his silver head
      To feel thee; thou shalt kiss the child asleep,
And dry the moistened curls that overspread
      His temples, while his breathing grows more deep:
And they who stand about the sick man's bed,
      Shall joy to listen to thy distant sweep,
And softly part his curtains to allow
Thy visit, grateful to his burning brow.

Go—but the circle of eternal change,
      Which is the life of nature, shall restore,
With sounds and scents from all thy mighty range
      Thee to thy birthplace of the deep once more;
Sweet odours in the sea-air, sweet and strange,
      Shall tell the home-sick mariner of the shore;
And, listening to thy murmur, he shall deem
He hears the rustling leaf and running stream.

An Autumn Sunset

Edith Wharton

I

Leaguered in fire
The wild black promontories of the coast extend
Their savage silhouettes;
The sun in universal carnage sets,
And, halting higher,
The motionless storm-clouds mass their sullen threats,
Like an advancing mob in sword-points penned,
That, balked, stands at bay.
Mid-zenith hangs the fascinated day
In wind-lustrated hollows crystalline,
A wan Valkyrie whose wide pinions shine
Across the ensanguined ruins of the fray,
And in her hand swings high o'erhead,
Above the waster of war,
The silver torch-light of the evening star
Wherewith to search the faces of the dead.

II

Lagooned in gold,
Seem not those jetty promontories rather
The outposts of some ancient land forlorn,
Uncomforted of morn,
Where old oblivions gather,
The melancholy unconsoling fold

Of all things that go utterly to death
And mix no more, no more
With life's perpetually awakening breath?
Shall Time not ferry me to such a shore,
Over such sailless seas,
To walk with hope's slain importunities
In miserable marriage? Nay, shall not
All things be there forgot,
Save the sea's golden barrier and the black
Close-crouching promontories?
Dead to all shames, forgotten of all glories,
Shall I not wander there, a shadow's shade,
A specter self-destroyed,
So purged of all remembrance and sucked back
Into the primal void,
That should we on the shore phantasmal meet
I should not know the coming of your feet?

November Evening

❧

L. M. Montgomery

Come, for the dusk is our own; let us fare forth together,
With a quiet delight in our hearts for the ripe, still,
    autumn weather,
Through the rustling valley and wood and over the
    crisping meadow,
Under a high-sprung sky, winnowed of mist and shadow.

Sharp is the frosty air, and through the far hill-gaps
    showing
Lucent sunset lakes of crocus and green are glowing;
'Tis the hour to walk at will in a wayward, unfettered
    roaming,
Caring for naught save the charm, elusive and swift, of
    the gloaming.

Watchful and stirless the fields as if not unkindly holding
Harvested joys in their clasp, and to their broad bosoms
    folding
Baby hopes of a Spring, trusted to motherly keeping,
Thus to be cherished and happed through the long
    months of their sleeping.

Silent the woods are and gray; but the firs than ever are
    greener,
Nipped by the frost till the tang of their loosened balsam
    is keener;

And one little wind in their boughs, eerily swaying and
    swinging,
Very soft and low, like a wandering minstrel is singing.

Beautiful is the year, but not as the springlike maiden
Garlanded with her hopes—rather the woman laden
With wealth of joy and grief, worthily won through
    living,
Wearing her sorrow now like a garment of praise and
    thanksgiving.

Gently the dark comes down over the wild, fair places,
The whispering glens in the hills, the open, starry
    spaces;
Rich with the gifts of the night, sated with questing
    and dreaming,
We turn to the dearest of paths where the star of the
    homelight is gleaming.

Night

Sonnet XXVII

William Shakespeare

Weary with toil, I haste me to my bed,
The dear repose for limbs with travel tir'd;
But then begins a journey in my head,
To work my mind, when body's work's expir'd:
For then my thoughts—from far where I abide—
Intend a zealous pilgrimage to thee,
And keep my drooping eyelids open wide,
Looking on darkness which the blind do see:
Save that my soul's imaginary sight
Presents thy shadow to my sightless view,
Which, like a jewel hung in ghastly night,
Makes black night beauteous and her old face new.
    Lo! Thus, by day my limbs, by night my mind,
    For thee, and for myself, no quiet find.

Evening Primrose

John Clare

When once the sun sinks in the west,
And dewdrops pearl the Evening's breast;
Almost as pale as moonbeams are,
Or its companionable star,
The evening primrose opes anew
Its delicate blossoms to the dew;
And, hermit-like, shunning the light,
Wastes its fair bloom upon the Night,
Who, blindfold to its fond caresses,
Knows not the beauty it possesses.
Thus it blooms on while night is by;
When day looks out with open eye,
'Bashed at the gaze it cannot shun,
It faints and withers and is gone.

The Evening-Watch

A Dialogue

Henry Vaughan

Body

Farewell! I go to sleep; but when
The day-star springs, I'll wake again.

Soul

Go, sleep in peace; and when thou liest
Unnumber'd in thy dust, when all this frame
Is but one dram, and what thou now descriest
    In sev'ral parts shall want a name,
Then may His peace be with thee, and each dust
Writ in His book, Who ne'er betray'd man's trust!

Body

Amen! but hark, ere we two stray
How many hours dost think 'till day?

Soul

Ah go; th'art weak, and sleepy. Heav'n
Is a plain watch, and without figures winds
All ages up; who drew this circle, even
    He fills it; days and hours are blinds.
Yet this take with thee. The last gasp of Time
Is thy first breath, and man's eternal prime.

Ode to Evening

William Collins

If aught of oaten stop, or past'ral song,
May hope, chaste Eve, to soothe thy modest ear,
    Like thy own solemn springs,
    Thy springs and dying gales,

O nymph reserv'd, while now the bright-hair'd sun
Sits in yon western tent, whose cloudy skirts,
    With brede ethereal wove,
    O'erhang his wavy bed:

Now air is hushed, save where the weak-ey'd bat
With short shrill shriek flits by on leathern wing,
    Or where the beetle winds
    His small but sullen horn:

As oft he rises 'midst the twilight path,
Against the pilgrim, borne in heedless hum:
    Now teach me, maid composed,
    To breathe some softened strain,

Whose numbers stealing thro' thy dark'ning vale
May not unseemly with its stillness suit,
    As musing slow, I hail
    Thy genial loved return!

For when thy folding-star arising shows
His paly circlet, at his warning lamp
  The fragrant Hours, and Elves
  Who slept in buds the day,

And many a Nymph who wreathes her brows with
    sedge,
And sheds the freshening dew, and lovelier still,
  The pensive Pleasures sweet
  Prepare thy shadowy car.

Then let me rove some wild and healthy scene;
Or find some ruin, 'midst its dreary dells
  Whose walls more awful nod
  By thy religious gleams.

Or, if chill blust'ring winds, or driving rain,
Prevent my willing feet, be mine the hut
  That from the mountain's side
  Views wilds, and swelling floods,

And hamlets brown, and dim-discover'd spires,
And hears their simple bell, and marks o'er all
  Thy dewy fingers draw
  The gradual dusky veil.

While Spring shall pour his showers, as oft he
    wont,
And bathe thy breathing tresses, meekest Eve;
  While Summer loves to sport
  Beneath thy lingering light;

While sallow Autumn fills thy lap with leaves;
Or Winter, yelling through the troublous air,
     Affrights thy shrinking train
     And rudely rends thy robes;

So long, regardful of thy quiet rule,
Shall Fancy, Friendship, Science, smiling Peace,
     Thy gentlest influence own,
     And love thy favourite name!

Aedh Wishes for the Cloths of Heaven

William Butler Yeats

Had I the heavens' embroidered cloths,
Enwrought with golden and silver light,
The blue and the dim and the dark cloths
Of night and light and the half light,
I would spread the cloths under your feet:
But I, being poor, have only my dreams;
I have spread my dreams under your feet;
Tread softly because you tread on my dreams.

The Dream

John Donne

Dear love, for nothing less than thee
Would I have broke this happy dream,
    It was a theme
For reason, much too strong for fantasy,
Therefore thou wak'd'st me wisely; yet
My dream thou brok'st not, but continued'st it.
Thou art so true that thoughts of thee suffice,
To make dreams truths, and fables histories;
Enter these arms, for since thou thought'st it best,
Not to dream all my dream, let's act the rest.

As lightning, or a taper's light,
Thine eyes, and not thy noise waked me;
    Yet I thought thee
(For thou lov'st truth) an angel, at first sight;
But when I saw thou saw'st my heart,
And knew'st my thoughts, beyond an angel's art,
When thou knew'st what I dreamt, when thou knew'st
    when
Excess of joy would wake me, and cam'st then,
I must confess, it could not choose but be
Profane, to think thee any thing but thee.

Coming and staying show'd thee, thee,
But rising makes me doubt, that now
    Thou art not thou.

That love is weak, where fear's as strong as he;
'Tis not all spirit, pure, and brave,
If mixture it of fear, shame, honour, have;
Perchance as torches which must ready be,
Men light and put out, so thou deal'st with me;
Thou cam'st to kindle, goest to come; then I
Will dream that hope again, but else would die.

Moonrise

Gerard Manley Hopkins

I awoke in the Midsummer not-to-call night, in the
    white and the walk of the morning:
The moon, dwindled and thinned to the fringe of a
    fingernail held to the candle,
Or paring of paradisaïcal fruit, lovely in waning but
    lustreless,
Stepped from the stool, drew back from the barrow, of
    dark Maenefa the mountain;
A cusp still clasped him, a fluke yet fanged him,
    entangled him, not quit utterly.
This was the prized, the desirable sight, unsought,
    presented so easily,
Parted me leaf and leaf, divided me, eyelid and eyelid
    of slumber.

In the night

Stephen Crane

In the night
Grey heavy clouds muffled the valleys,
And the peaks looked toward God alone.
"O Master that movest the wind with a finger,
Humble, idle, futile peaks are we.
Grant that we may run swiftly across the world
To huddle in worship at Thy feet."

In the morning
A noise of men at work came the clear blue miles,
And the little black cities were apparent.
"O Master that knowest the meaning of raindrops,
Humble, idle, futile peaks are we.
Give voice to us, we pray, O Lord,
That we may sing Thy goodness to the sun."

In the evening
The far valleys were sprinkled with tiny lights.
"O Master,
Thou that knowest the value of kings and birds,
Thou hast made us humble, idle futile peaks.
Thou only needest eternal patience;
We bow to Thy wisdom, O Lord—
Humble, idle, futile peaks."

In the night
Grey heavy clouds muffled the valleys,
And the peaks looked toward God alone.

Mutability

Percy Bysshe Shelley

I

We are as clouds that veil the midnight moon;
    How restlessly they speed and gleam and quiver,
Streaking the darkness radiantly! yet soon
    Night closes round, and they are lost for ever:—

II

Or like forgotten lyres whose dissonant strings
    Give various response to each varying blast,
To whose frail frame no second motion brings
    One mood or modulation like the last.

III

We rest—a dream has power to poison sleep;
    We rise—one wandering thought pollutes the day;
We feel, conceive or reason, laugh or weep,
    Embrace fond woe, or cast our cares away:—

IV

It is the same!—For, be it joy or sorrow,
    The path of its departure still is free;
Man's yesterday may ne'er be like his morrow;
    Nought may endure but Mutability.

To Sleep

John Keats

O soft embalmer of the still midnight,
   Shutting, with careful fingers and benign,
Our gloom-pleas'd eyes, embower'd from the light,
   Enshaded in forgetfulness divine:
O soothest Sleep! if so it please thee, close
   In midst of this thine hymn my willing eyes,
Or wait the "Amen," ere thy poppy throws
   Around my bed its lulling charities.
Then save me, or the passed day will shine
Upon my pillow, breeding many woes,—
   Save me from curious conscience, that still lords
Its strength for darkness, burrowing like a mole;
   Turn the key deftly in the oiled wards,
And seal the hushed casket of my soul.

Frost at Midnight

❧

Samuel Taylor Coleridge

The Frost performs its secret ministry,
Unhelped by any wind. The owlet's cry
Came loud—and hark, again! loud as before.
The inmates of my cottage, all at rest,
Have left me to that solitude, which suits
Abstruser musings: save that at my side
My cradled infant slumbers peacefully.
'Tis calm indeed! so calm, that it disturbs
And vexes meditation with its strange
And extreme silentness. Sea, hill, and wood,
This populous village! Sea, and hill, and wood,
With all the numberless goings-on of life,
Inaudible as dreams! the thin blue flame
Lies on my low-burnt fire, and quivers not;
Only that film, which fluttered on the grate,
Still flutters there, the sole unquiet thing.
Methinks, its motion in this hush of nature
Gives it dim sympathies with me who live,
Making it a companionable form,
Whose puny flaps and freaks the idling Spirit
By its own moods interprets, every where

Echo or mirror seeking of itself,
And makes a toy of Thought.

But O! how oft,
How oft, at school, with most believing mind,
Presageful, have I gazed upon the bars,
To watch that fluttering stranger! and as oft
With unclosed lids, already had I dreamt
Of my sweet birth-place, and the old
        church-tower,
Whose bells, the poor man's only music, rang
From morn to evening, all the hot Fair-day,
So sweetly, that they stirred and haunted me
With a wild pleasure, falling on mine ear
Most like articulate sounds of things to come!
So gazed I, till the soothing things, I dreamt,
Lulled me to sleep, and sleep prolonged my
        dreams!
And so I brooded all the following morn,
Awed by the stern preceptor's face, mine eye
Fixed with mock study on my swimming book:
Save if the door half opened, and I snatched
A hasty glance, and still my heart leaped up,
For still I hoped to see the stranger's face,
Townsman, or aunt, or sister more beloved,
My play-mate when we both were clothed alike!

Dear Babe, that sleepest cradled by my side,
Whose gentle breathings, heard in this deep
    calm,
Fill up the intersperséd vacancies
And momentary pauses of the thought!
My babe so beautiful! it thrills my heart
With tender gladness, thus to look at thee,
And think that thou shalt learn far other lore,
And in far other scenes! For I was reared
In the great city, pent 'mid cloisters dim,
And saw nought lovely but the sky and stars.
But thou, my babe! shalt wander like a breeze
By lakes and sandy shores, beneath the crags
Of ancient mountain, and beneath the clouds,
Which image in their bulk both lakes and shores
And mountain crags: so shalt thou see and hear
The lovely shapes and sounds intelligible
Of that eternal language, which thy God
Utters, who from eternity doth teach
Himself in all, and all things in himself.
Great universal Teacher! he shall mould
Thy spirit, and by giving make it ask.

    Therefore all seasons shall be sweet to thee,
Whether the summer clothe the general earth
With greenness, or the redbreast sit and sing

Betwixt the tufts of snow on the bare branch
Of mossy apple-tree, while the night-thatch
Smokes in the sun-thaw; whether the eave-drops
    fall
Heard only in the trances of the blast,
Or if the secret ministry of frost
Shall hang them up in silent icicles,
Quietly shining to the quiet Moon.

Darkest Night

Before Marching and After

Thomas Hardy

Orion swung southward aslant
Where the starved Egdon pine-trees had thinned,
The Pleiads aloft seemed to pant
With the heather that twitched in the wind;
But he looked on indifferent to sights such as these,
Unswayed by love, friendship, home joy or home sorrow,
And wondered to what he would march on the morrow.

The crazed household-clock with its whirr
Rang midnight within as he stood,
He heard the low sighing of her
Who had striven from his birth for his good;
But he still only asked the spring starlight, the breeze,
What great thing or small thing his history would borrow
From that Game with Death he would play on the morrow.

When the heath wore the robe of late summer,
And the fuchsia-bells, hot in the sun,
Hung red by the door, a quick comer
Brought tidings that marching was done
For him who had joined in that game overseas
Where Death stood to win, though his name was to borrow
A brightness therefrom not to fade on the morrow.

Darkness

George Gordon, Lord Byron

I had a dream, which was not all a dream.
The bright sun was extinguish'd, and the stars
Did wander darkling in the eternal space,
Rayless, and pathless, and the icy earth
Swung blind and blackening in the moonless air;
Morn came and went—and came, and brought no day,
And men forgot their passions in the dread
Of this their desolation; and all hearts
Were chill'd into a selfish prayer for light:
And they did live by watchfires—and the thrones,
The palaces of crowned kings—the huts,
The habitations of all things which dwell,
Were burnt for beacons; cities were consum'd,
And men were gather'd round their blazing homes
To look once more into each other's face;
Happy were those who dwelt within the eye
Of the volcanos, and their mountain-torch:
A fearful hope was all the world contain'd;
Forests were set on fire—but hour by hour
They fell and faded—and the crackling trunks
Extinguish'd with a crash—and all was black.
The brows of men by the despairing light
Wore an unearthly aspect, as by fits
The flashes fell upon them; some lay down
And hid their eyes and wept; and some did rest
Their chins upon their clenched hands, and smil'd;

And others hurried to and fro, and fed
Their funeral piles with fuel, and look'd up
With mad disquietude on the dull sky,
The pall of a past world; and then again
With curses cast them down upon the dust,
And gnash'd their teeth and howl'd: the wild birds shriek'd
And, terrified, did flutter on the ground,
And flap their useless wings; the wildest brutes
Came tame and tremulous; and vipers crawl'd
And twin'd themselves among the multitude,
Hissing, but stingless—they were slain for food.
And War, which for a moment was no more,
Did glut himself again:—a meal was bought
With blood, and each sate sullenly apart
Gorging himself in gloom: no love was left;
All earth was but one thought—and that was death
Immediate and inglorious; and the pang
Of famine fed upon all entrails—men
Died, and their bones were tombless as their flesh;
The meagre by the meagre were devour'd,
Even dogs assail'd their masters, all save one,
And he was faithful to a corse, and kept
The birds and beasts and famish'd men at bay,
Till hunger clung them, or the dropping dead
Lured their lank jaws; himself sought out no food,
But with a piteous and perpetual moan,
And a quick desolate cry, licking the hand
Which answer'd not with a caress—he died.
The crowd was famish'd by degrees; but two
Of an enormous city did survive,
And they were enemies: they met beside
The dying embers of an altar-place

Where had been heap'd a mass of holy things
For an unholy usage; they raked up,
And shivering scrap'd with their cold skeleton hands
The feeble ashes, and their feeble breath
Blew for a little life, and made a flame
Which was a mockery; then they lifted up
Their eyes as it grew lighter, and beheld
Each other's aspects—saw, and shriek'd, and died—
Even of their mutual hideousness they died,
Unknowing who he was upon whose brow
Famine had written Fiend. The world was void,
The populous and the powerful was a lump,
Seasonless, herbless, treeless, manless, lifeless—
A lump of death—a chaos of hard clay.
The rivers, lakes and ocean all stood still,
And nothing stirr'd within their silent depths;
Ships sailorless lay rotting on the sea,
And their masts fell down piecemeal: as they dropp'd
They slept on the abyss without a surge—
The waves were dead; the tides were in their grave,
The moon, their mistress, had expired before;
The winds were wither'd in the stagnant air,
And the clouds perish'd; Darkness had no need
Of aid from them—She was the Universe.

Ulalume—A Ballad

Edgar Allan Poe

The skies they were ashen and sober;
    The leaves they were crispéd and sere—
    The leaves they were withering and sere:
It was night, in the lonesome October
    Of my most immemorial year:
It was hard by the dim lake of Auber,
    In the misty mid region of Weir:—
It was down by the dank tarn of Auber,
    In the ghoul-haunted woodland of Weir.

Here once, through an alley Titanic,
    Of cypress, I roamed with my Soul—
    Of cypress, with Psyche, my Soul.
These were days when my heart was volcanic
    As the scoriac rivers that roll—
    As the lavas that restlessly roll
Their sulphurous currents down Yaanek,
    In the ultimate climes of the Pole—
That groan as they roll down Mount Yaanek
    In the realms of the Boreal Pole.

Our talk had been serious and sober,
    But our thoughts they were palsied and sere—
    Our memories were treacherous and sere;
For we knew not the month was October,
    And we marked not the night of the year—

(Ah, night of all nights in the year!)
We noted not the dim lake of Auber,
    (Though once we had journeyed down here)—
We remembered not the dank tarn of Auber,
    Nor the ghoul-haunted woodland of Weir.

And now, as the night was senescent,
    And star-dials pointed to morn—
    As the star-dials hinted of morn—
At the end of our path a liquescent
    And nebulous lustre was born
Out of which a miraculous crescent
    Arose with a duplicate horn—
Astarte's bediamonded crescent,
    Distinct with its duplicate horn.

And I said—"She is warmer than Dian;
    She rolls through an ether of sighs—
    She revels in a region of sighs.
She has seen that the tears are not dry on
    These cheeks where the worm never dies,
And has come past the stars of the Lion,
    To point us the path to the skies—
    To the Lethean peace of the skies—
Come up, in despite of the Lion,
    To shine on us with her bright eyes—
Come up, through the lair of the Lion,
    With love in her luminous eyes."

But Psyche, uplifting her finger,
    Said: "Sadly this star I mistrust—

Her pallor I strangely mistrust—
Ah, hasten!—ah, let us not linger!
   Ah, fly!—let us fly!—for we must."
In terror she spoke; letting sink her
   Wings till they trailed in the dust—
In agony sobbed; letting sink her
   Plumes till they trailed in the dust—
   Till they sorrowfully trailed in the dust.

I replied—"This is nothing but dreaming.
   Let us on, by this tremulous light!
   Let us bathe in this crystalline light!
Its Sybillic splendor is beaming
   With Hope and in Beauty to-night—
   See!—it flickers up the sky through the night!
Ah, we safely may trust to its gleaming
   And be sure it will lead us aright—
We safely may trust to a gleaming
   That cannot but guide us aright
   Since it flickers up to Heaven through the night."

Thus I pacified Psyche and kissed her,
   And tempted her out of her gloom—
   And conquered her scruples and gloom;
And we passed to the end of the vista—
   But were stopped by the door of a tomb—
   By the door of a legended tomb:—
And I said—"What is written, sweet sister,
   On the door of this legended tomb?"
   She replied—"Ulalume—Ulalume!—
   'T is the vault of thy lost Ulalume!"

Then my heart it grew ashen and sober
　　As the leaves that were crispéd and sere—
　　As the leaves that were withering and sere—
And I cried—"It was surely October,
　　On *this* very night of last year,
　　That I journeyed—I journeyed down here!—
　　That I brought a dread burden down here—
　　On this night, of all nights in the year,
　　Ah, what demon hath tempted me here?
Well I know, now, this dim lake of Auber—
　　This misty mid region of Weir:—
Well I know, now, this dank tarn of Auber—
　　This ghoul-haunted woodland of Weir."

Said we, then,—the two, then,—"Ah, can it
　　Have been that the woodlandish ghouls—
　　The pitiful, the merciful ghouls,
To bar up our way and to ban it
　　From the secret that lies in these wolds—
　　From the thing that lies hidden in these wolds—
Have drawn up the spectre of a planet
　　From the limbo of lunary souls—
This sinfully scintillant planet
　　From the Hell of planetary souls?"

Despair

H. P. Lovecraft

O'er the midnight moorlands crying,
Thro' the cypress forests sighing,
In the night-wind madly flying,
      Hellish forms with streaming hair;
In the barren branches creaking,
By the stagnant swamp-pools speaking,
Past the shore-cliffs ever shrieking;
      Damn'd daemons of despair.

Once, I think I half remember,
Ere the grey skies of November
Quench'd my youth's aspiring ember,
      Liv'd there such a thing as bliss;
Skies that now are dark were beaming,
Gold and azure, splendid seeming
Till I learn'd it all was dreaming—
      Deadly drowsiness of Dis.

But the stream of Time, swift flowing,
Brings the torment of half-knowing—
Dimly rushing, blindly going
      Past the never-trodden lea;
And the voyager, repining,
Sees the wicked death-fires shining,
Hears the wicked petrel's whining
      As he helpless drifts to sea.

Evil wings in ether beating;
Vultures at the spirit eating;
Things unseen forever fleeting
        Black against the leering sky.
Ghastly shades of bygone gladness,
Clawing fiends of future sadness,
Mingle in a cloud of madness
        Ever on the soul to lie.

Thus the living, lone and sobbing,
In the throes of anguish throbbing,
With the loathsome Furies robbing
        Night and noon of peace and rest.
But beyond the groans and grating
Of abhorrent Life, is waiting
Sweet Oblivion, culminating
        All the years of fruitless quest.

The Nightmare

W. S. Gilbert

When you're lying awake with a dismal headache,
    and repose is taboo'd by anxiety,
I conceive you may use any language you choose to
    indulge in without impropriety;
For your brain is on fire—the bedclothes conspire of
    usual slumber to plunder you:
First your counterpane goes and uncovers your toes,
    and your sheet slips demurely from under you;
Then the blanketing tickles—you feel like mixed pickles,
    so terribly sharp is the pricking,
And you're hot, and you're cross, and you tumble
    and toss till there's nothing 'twixt you and the
    ticking.
Then the bedclothes all creep to the ground in a heap,
    and you pick 'em all up in a tangle;
Next your pillow resigns and politely declines to remain
    at its usual angle!
Well, you get some repose in the form of a doze, with
    hot eyeballs and head ever aching,
But your slumbering teems with such horrible dreams
    that you'd very much better be waking;
For you dream you are crossing the Channel, and
    tossing about in a steamer from Harwich,
Which is something between a large bathing-machine
    and a very small second-class carriage;

And you're giving a treat (penny ice and cold meat) to
a party of friends and relations—
They're a ravenous horde—and they all came on
board at Sloane Square and South Kensington
Stations.
And bound on that journey you find your attorney
(who started that morning from Devon);
He's a bit undersized, and you don't feel surprised
when he tells you he's only eleven.
Well, you're driving like mad with this singular lad
(by the bye the ship's now a four-wheeler),
And you're playing round games, and he calls you bad
names when you tell him that "ties pay the dealer";
But this you can't stand, so you throw up your hand,
and you find you're as cold as an icicle,
In your shirt and your socks (the black silk with gold
clocks), crossing Salisbury Plain on a bicycle:
And he and the crew are on bicycles too—which they've
somehow or other invested in—
And he's telling the tars all the particulars of a company
he's interested in—
It's a scheme of devices, to get at low prices, all goods
from cough mixtures to cables
(Which tickled the sailors) by treating retailers, as though
they were all vegetables—
You get a good spadesman to plant a small tradesman
(first take off his boots with a boot-tree),
And his legs will take root, and his fingers will shoot,
and they'll blossom and bud like a fruit-tree—
From the greengrocer tree you get grapes and green
pea, cauliflower, pineapple, and cranberries,

While the pastry-cook plant cherry-brandy will grant—
    apple puffs, and three-corners, and banberries—
The shares are a penny, and ever so many are taken
    by ROTHSCHILD and BARING,
And just as a few are allotted to you, you awake with
    a shudder despairing—
You're a regular wreck, with a crick in your neck,
    and no wonder you snore, for your head's on the
    floor, and you've needles and pins from your soles
    to your shins, and your flesh is a-creep, for your
    left leg's asleep, and you've cramp in your toes,
    and a fly on your nose, and some fluff in your
    lung, and a feverish tongue, and a thirst that's
    intense, and a general sense that you haven't
    been sleeping in clover;
But the darkness has passed, and it's daylight at last, and
    the night has been long—ditto, ditto my song—and
    thank goodness they're both of them over!

Signature Select Classics

Elegantly Designed Booklets of Poetry and Prose

This book is part of Sterling Publishing's Signature Select Classics chapbook series. Each booklet features distinguished poetry and prose by the world's greatest poets and writers in an elegantly designed and printed chapbook binding. These books are essential reading for lovers of classic literature and collectible editions in their own right. They make perfect keepsakes to own and to share with others.